Southern Favorite Recipes

E. Harp

VOLUME II

Willorene Morrow

Copyright © 2010

by

Willorene Morrow

ISBN: 978-0-942407-99-0

Manufactured in the United States of America

Special thanks to Sandra Carter for all her help in
compiling and typing this book.

**FATHER
&
SON**
PUBLISHING, INC.
4909 N. Monroe Street • Tallahassee, Florida 32303
http://www.fatherson.com email: lance@fatherson.com
800-741-2712

DEDICATION

I dedicate this book to my husband, Jerry Morrow, the love of my life. May he rest in peace.

To my son, Duane Morrow, I wish every mama could know the joy of having a son as special as he.

Table of Contents

PREFACE

Exchanging recipes has long been a tradition of good cooks. The recipes in this book have been exchanged by many good cooks who frequented the Beauty Nook beauty salon in Reynolds, Georgia for many years.

The fact that these are home recipes used by good cooks of the south gives the book an additional value. If you are entertaining a large group or feeding the family on a typical day, you will find this book has everything you need to serve a delightful meal.

ESCAPE

From the world and all it turmoil
As my mixer beats the cake
and the pot on the stove boils

Into my kitchen, all the tensions
And pressures of life, I take.

Some are my own!
May I have your attention!

Some came from afar:
Some from friends I did so
willingly take.

Over the years, I've collected this completion

And enjoyed the time spent in my
kitchen, as I from the world did
ESCAPE.

By
Willorene Morrow

APPETIZERS
and
BEVERAGES

Index

APPETIZERS

BLACK BEAN DIP

1   8 ounce package cream cheese
1   8 ounce package sour cream
1   can black beans, do not drain
1   package taco seasoning mix

Mix all ingredients together adding just enough sour cream to make the mixture "dippable." Serve with Tostitos Scoops.

BLT DIP

2   packages Hormel original Real Bacon Bits
1   cup sour cream
1   cup mayonnaise
Iceberg lettuce, shredded fine
tomatoes, chopped fine

Combine sour cream and mayonnaise and one package of bacon bits. Mix well and layer in bottom of 9 x 13 inch dish. Layer shredded lettuce. Layer tomatoes on top of lettuce. Sprinkle ½ package of bacon bits on top. Serve with bagel bites.

BROCCOLI DIP

1   stick butter
1   10¾ ounce can cream of mushroom soup
2   rolls Kraft garlic cheese
1   onion, chopped
1   can chopped mushrooms, drained
2   10 ounce packages chopped frozen broccoli

> Cook and drain broccoli, no salt. Saute onions in butter, add soup, mushrooms, cheese and broccoli. Heat well and serve with large fritos or crackers.

CHEESE BALL

2   8 ounce packages cream cheese
2   tablespoons onion
¼   cup green bell pepper, chopped
1   15 ounce can crushed pineapple, drained
1   cup pecans, chopped

> Mix all ingredients together. Shape into a ball and chill.

CHEESE STRAWS

2 cups sharp cheese, grated
½ cup butter
2 teaspoons baking powder
2 cups plain flour
½ teaspoon salt
¼ teaspoon red pepper

Measure flour after sifting once. Cream cheese and butter. Add the other ingredients. Run through press onto cookie sheet and bake at 450 degrees 8-10 minutes or until light brown around edges.

CHEESE WAFERS

1½ sticks butter
2 cups grated sharp cheese
¼ teaspoon red pepper
2 cups plain flour
1 dash salt
2 cups Rice Krispies
1 cup chopped pecans

Cream butter until soft and fluffy. Add other ingredients to butter and blend well. Drop by teaspoon or roll into small balls, on an ungreased cookie sheet. Flatten with a moistened fork. Bake at 350 degrees for 15 minutes. Store in airtight container.

CHICKEN WINGS ORIENTAL

2   pounds chicken wings
1   teaspoon garlic salt
1   teaspoon parsley
½   teaspoon thyme
¼   teaspoon basil leaves
1   cup soy sauce

Marinate chicken at least two hours in remaining ingredients. Broil 10 minutes on each side on top rack of oven.

COCKTAIL MEATBALLS

1   bottle "Heinz" chili sauce
juice of 1 lemon
1   6 ounce jar grape jelly
½   cup crushed cornflakes
1   grated clove of garlic
2   beaten eggs
2   pounds ground beef
salt and pepper

Combine first 3 ingredients in a saucepan and melt over low heat. Mix the last 6 ingredients and form into small meatballs. Drop meatballs into sauce and simmer 1 hour. *DO NOT BROWN MEATBALLS.*

CRAB MEAT APPETIZER

1   can crab meat
1   package 6 English muffins
2   tablespoons Miracle Whip or mayonnaise
1   stick butter
1   jar Kraft Old English Cheese
dash garlic salt or juice

Have above ingredients at room temperature. Blend together. Slice muffins in half. Spread with mixture. Freeze. Take out and cut each into eighths. Put in plastic bag and freeze. When ready to serve, bake on cookie sheet at 400 degrees till brown and bubbly.

CUCUMBER SANDWICH SPREAD

3   3 ounce packages cream cheese
1   tablespoon heavy cream
¾   cup grated cucumber
1   teaspoon grated onion
dash Tabasco

Mix all ingredients well. Spread on bread.

DEVILED CHEESE SPREAD

1	8 ounce package cream cheese
2	hard boiled eggs, chopped
1	small onion, chopped
¼	teaspoon salt
3	2 ounce jars, chopped pimento or 1 green pepper diced
½	teaspoon paprika
4	tablespoons mayonnaise

Mix all ingredients well. Spread on rye bread.

GRANOLA

8-10 cups 1-Minute Quick Cook Quaker Oats

½	cup honey
3	cups soft, dark brown sugar
3	sticks butter
1	cup coconut flakes
1	cup raisins

Melt butter in a large pan. Add sugar and honey. Stir in oats and coconut. Add enough oats to soak up all the sugar mixture and try not to have the sugar mixture too wet. Add raisins. Spread mixture onto two baking sheets. Bake at 375 degrees till brown and drying, about 20-30 minutes. Turn oat mixture 3 times during cooking time using a fork to break into lumps.

HOT ARTICHOKE DIP

2   14 ounce cans artichoke hearts
2   cups grated Parmesan cheese
2   cups Hellman's mayonnaise
½   cup green onion tops only
¼   teaspoon garlic powder
¼   teaspoon Tabasco sauce
¼   teaspoon Worcestershire sauce
paprika

> Drain artichokes and cut into small pieces. Mix all ingredients together and put into casserole dish. Sprinkle with paprika. Bake at 350 degrees for 20 - 30 minutes. Serve with crackers or vegetable sticks.

JALAPENO PEPPER SQUARES

8   ounce Jalapeno pepper slices, seeds removed
10 ounce sharp Cheddar cheese, grated
8   ounce sliced green olives
4   eggs, beaten

> Lay peppers and olives in 9 x 13 inch dish. Arrange grated cheese on top. Pour beaten eggs over top. Bake at 350 degrees for 40-45 minutes until lightly browned. Cut in squares and serve.

JOHN WAYNE CASSEROLE

2   4 ounce cans chopped green chili's
1   pound Monterey Jack cheese, grated
1   pound Cheddar cheese, grated
4   egg whites (reserve yolks for later use)
⅔   cup evaporated milk
1   tablespoon flour
½   teaspoon salt
⅛   teaspoon pepper
2   medium tomatoes, sliced

Preheat oven to 325 degrees. Combine cheeses and chili's. Turn into well greased shallow 2 quart casserole dish (12 x 8 x 2 inch). In a large bowl, beat egg whites until stiff peaks form. In another bowl, combine yolks, milk, flour, salt and pepper. Mix until well blended. Using a rubber scraper, gently fold egg whites into egg yolk mixture. Pour this mixture over cheeses. With a fork, ooze it through the cheeses. Bake for 30 minutes. Remove and arrange tomato slices on top. Bake 30 minutes longer. Serve hot.

MEXICAN DIP

3   fresh tomatoes, diced
3   green onions, chopped
1   can black olives, pitted and sliced
1   small can green chilies, chopped
3   tablespoons olive oil
1½ teaspoons vinegar
1   teaspoon garlic salt

Mix all ingredients thoroughly. Refrigerate several hours and serve with corn chips.

MINI SALTINE MIX

1   box mini premium saltines
½   bottle dill weed
1   package dry ranch style dressing mix
½   cup canola oil
Creole seasoning to taste

> Mix together and bake on cookie sheet for 20 - 30 minutes at
> 200 degrees. Stir every 10 minutes.

NUT SNACKERS

1   egg white
¾   cup brown sugar
2   tablespoons sifted self rising flour
½   teaspoon vanilla
2   cups pecan halves

> Heat oven to 250 degrees. Beat egg white until it stands in soft
> peaks. Mix in brown sugar, flour and vanilla. Fold in pecans,
> coating well. Place pecans on greased cookie sheet 1 inch apart.
> Bake for 30 minutes. Turn off oven and let stand in oven for 30
> more minutes. Take out, cool on pan, store in airtight container.
> Freezes well.

NUTS AND BOLTS

4	cups Rice Chex
4	cups Wheat Chex
4	cups Corn Chex or Cheerios
1	can salted peanuts
1	can mixed nuts
1	can pecans
1	small bag of pretzel sticks
½	pounds melted margarine
2	tablespoons Worcestershire sauce
2	tablespoons garlic salt

Mix cereals, nuts, and pretzels in large shallow baking pan. Combine remaining ingredients and pour over cereal mixture. Mix well. Heat in 250 degree oven for 1 hour, stir often. Cool thoroughly and store in moisture proof containers.

OLIVE-CHEESE BALLS

1	cup Cheddar cheese, grated
½	cup all purpose flour
¼	cup butter, softened
½	teaspoon paprika
¼	teaspoon salt
3	dozen pimento-stuffed olives

dash cayenne pepper

Combine first 6 ingredients and blend together well. Drain olives well on paper towels. Shape a thin layer of cheese mixture around each olive: place on ungreased cookie sheet. Bake at 425 degrees for 8-10 minutes or until lightly browned.

OYSTER CRACKER MIX

2	bags oyster crackers	½	cup canola oil
½	bottle dill weed		Creole seasoning to taste
1	package dry ranch style dressing mix		

Mix together and bake on cookie sheet for 20-30 minutes at 200 degrees. Stir every 10 minutes.

PARTY CHEESE BALL

½   pounds sharp Cheddar cheese, grated
½   pounds mild Cheddar cheese, grated
2   pounds cream cheese
1   2 ounce can ripe olives, chopped
1   cup chopped pecans
2   cloves garlic, minced
½   teaspoon salt
½   cup evaporated milk

Mix all ingredients well. Shape into ball or 2 rolls. Sprinkle with paprika. Wrap with waxed paper and foil. Refrigerate. Slice as needed and serve with crackers.

PARTY DIP

1	pound Velveeta cheese	1	pound sausage, ground
1	pound hamburger meat	1	16 ounce jar of salsa

Brown hamburger meat and sausage. Cut cheese into cubes. Put meat and cheese in a crock pot with salsa. Cook on high until cheese is melted and reduce temperature to low. Serve warm with Fritos Scoops.

PIMENTO CHEESE

1   pound sharp Cheddar cheese, grated very fine
2   2 ounce jars chopped pimento
1   cup Kraft mayonnaise
black pepper to taste
garlic salt to taste

> Mix cheese, pimento, garlic salt and pepper. Add mayonnaise to spreading consistency. If you would like to "spice it up", add ¼ cup chopped Jalapeno peppers or ½ teaspoon Cayenne pepper.

PIMENTO CHEESE SPREAD

1   12 ounce can evaporated milk
1   pound Cheddar cheese, cut up
2   tablespoons vinegar
½   level teaspoon dry mustard
1   7 ounce jar chopped pimentos, drained
½   teaspoon salt
dash cayenne pepper

> Heat milk in double boiler, add cheese to hot milk and stir until smooth. Add remaining ingredients. May be stored in refrigerator for weeks.

SAUSAGE CHEESE BALLS

3   cups Bisquick mix
2   cups sharp cheese, grated
1   pound mild sausage, or hot if preferred

Mix all ingredients together. If too thick, add water. Make small 1 inch balls and bake in 350 degree over for 15-20 minutes.

SAUSAGE PINWHEELS

1   can refrigerated biscuits
1   pound hot sausage

On floured board roll each biscuit out thin: cover with raw sausage and roll up. Chill before cutting into thin slices. Place on ungreased cookie sheet and bake at 375 degrees until brown and crisp. Yields: 5-6 dozens.

SHRIMP DIP

1   8 ounce package cream cheese, softened
1   8 ounce can shrimp, chopped
1   tablespoon Worcestershire sauce
¼   teaspoon garlic powder
2   tablespoons mayonnaise
1   8 ounce carton sour cream

Mix all ingredients until well blended. Serve with crackers or raw vegetables.

SHRIMP MOLD

1   8 ounce package cream cheese
1   3 ounce package cream cheese
2   cans shrimp, deveined and chopped

   Drain water from shrimp and bring to a boil.

2   envelopes Knox gelatin
½   cup cold water
¼   cup lemon juice
1   cup mayonnaise
1   cup chopped celery
½   clove garlic
1   jar pimento
Tabasco as desired

   Soften gelatin in the ½ cup cold water. Add gelatin and softened cream cheese to hot shrimp water. Mix well. Add all other
   ingredients. Pour in mold and refrigerate to congeal. Yields:
   2 molds.

SHRIMP SALAD

2   16 ounce cans shrimp, chopped
¼   cup chopped pimento
1   8 ounce package cream cheese, softened
¼   cup finely chopped green onions
mayonnaise

   Mix all ingredients: add enough mayonnaise to form a smooth
   mixture.

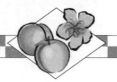

SOMBRERO DIP

1   pound hamburger, brown in small amount of oil
1   tablespoon chili powder
½   cup minced onion
1   clove garlic, minced
1   teaspoon salt
½   cup hot ketchup
1   can refried beans
1   can Jalapeno bean dip
2   cups sharp Cheddar cheese, grated
½   cup sliced green olives

Mix all ingredients (except olives) together and simmer for 30 minutes. Remove from heat and fold in ½ cup sliced green olives. Place in a chafing dish. Sprinkle 2 cups grated sharp Cheddar cheese and minced onion around the edge. Serve with Fritos.

SPINACH DIP

1   10 ounce package frozen chopped spinach, thawed
1   8 ounce carton sour cream
1   cup mayonnaise
1   package Knorr Dry Vegetable Soup mix
1   8 ounce can sliced water chestnuts
3   green onions, chopped

Squeeze spinach dry. Stir together all ingredients. Cover and refrigerate. Serve with crackers or chips.

SPREAD FOR SWEET SANDWICH

1   20 ounce can crushed pineapple, drained
1   cup finely ground raisins
1   cup pecans, chopped
1   cup sugar
1   stick butter
2   eggs

> Put eggs, sugar, and butter in heavy pan and cook until thick. Add pecans and raisins while mixture is hot. Cool. Add pineapple. If using all at once, mix in mayonnaise. If not, spread bread when making sandwich.

STRAWBERRY CONFECTION

3   3 ounce packages strawberry Jello
1   cup nuts chopped fine
1   can sweetened condensed milk
1   cup flaked coconut

> Mix all ingredients and place in plastic bowl. Seal and store in refrigerator 24 hours. Roll into small balls and shape in form of strawberries. Roll in red sugar, available in most grocery stores in small container. Pieces of green candied cherries, slivers of almonds or purchased stems may be inserted in broad end of strawberry to resemble stems. Store in refrigerator. Will keep for months.

WALKING TACO

1 can Jalapeno bean dip

8 ounces sour cream

8 ounces cream cheese

1 package Taco seasoning mix

2-3 avocados

1 package guacamole dip mix

1 jar Pace Thick and Chunky Picante Sauce

3-4 green onions, including tops finely chopped

1-2 tomatoes, finely chopped

8 ounces Cheddar cheese, shredded

Mix sour cream, cream cheese and taco seasoning mix together. Mix avocados and guacamole dip, mix together. Then combine all ingredients and mix well. Garnish with hot peppers and black olives. Serve with tortilla chips.

WATERCRESS AND DRIED BEEF SPREAD

1 2.75 ounce jar dried beef, chopped

boiling water

2 tablespoons mayonnaise

1 tablespoon prepared horseradish

4 ounces soft cream cheese

½ cup finely chopped watercress

Chop the dried beef and watercress with a french knife or kitchen scissors. Place dried beef in a wire strainer and pour boiling water through it. Drain well. Beat mayonnaise, horseradish and cream cheese until fluffy. Fold in dried beef and watercress. Yields: about 1 cup. Serve with crackers.

BEVERAGES

CRANBERRY PUNCH

2   pints cranberry juice
1   12 ounce can frozen lemonade + 2 cans water
1   12 ounce can frozen orange juice + 1 can water
1   quart gingerale

Mix all ingredients except gingerale. Freeze ice mold of fruit juices and float in punch bowl. Add gingerale just before serving.

GOLDEN PUNCH

2   6 ounce cans frozen orange juice
2   6 ounce cans frozen lemonade concentrate
2   12 ounce cans apricot nectar
2   18 ounce cans pineapple juice

Add water to frozen concentrates as directed. Combine with the apricot nectar and pineapple juice. Chill. Yields: 6 quarts or about 50 servings. NOTE: This cantaloupe colored punch is one of the simplest of all to prepare. Its full, rich flavor can stand diluting, slightly, with decorative ice cubes or an ice block.

GOOD FRUIT PUNCH

1   gallon water

5   pounds sugar

3   48 ounce cans pineapple juice

1   large bottle lemon juice

3   tablespoons almond flavoring

4   quarts gingerale

> Mix all ingredients except gingerale. Freeze in wide mouth containers. Take out of freezer several hours before serving. Chip with ice pick. Put in punch bowl and add gingerale just before serving.

GREAT GRANDDADDY'S EGGNOG

1   dozen eggs, separated

1¼ cup bourbon

1   quart whipping cream

3   tablespoons sugar

½   cup sugar + 1 tablespoon

nutmeg

> Beat egg yolks for 20 minutes on medium speed of mixer, until they are light lemoned colored, stiff and fluffy. Continue beating and add bourbon a drop at a time. Whip cream until it stands in peaks: add 3 tablespoons sugar. Fold egg yolk mixture into whipped cream. Beat egg whites until they are dry and have completely lost their gloss before you start adding sugar. This step is important: it is the secret of the eggnog's standing up quality. Add the ½ cup sugar 1 tablespoon at a time. Continue beating for about 10 minutes after all sugar has been added. Fold the beaten egg whites into the cream and egg yolk mixture, continuing to blend with a folding motion until it is well mixed and smooth. Sprinkle each glass with nutmeg.

HOT COCOA MIX

1   1 pound package instant cocoa
1   cup sifted confectioners sugar
1   7 ounce jar non dairy coffee creamer
1   24 ounce package instant non fat dry milk

> Thoroughly mix all ingredients. To serve, combine ⅓ cup dry mix and 1 cup hot water. Top each serving with marshmallow and use peppermint or cinnamon stick as stirrer. Yields: approximately 4 quarts.

HOT PUNCH

2   quarts cranberry juice
4   quarts apple juice
1   cup brown sugar
6-8 cinnamon sticks
1   tablespoon cloves

> Pour juices in kettle and heat. Place sugar, cinnamon sticks and cloves in a steeping bag and tie. Place bag in hot juice and let stand for 20 minutes before serving.

INSTANT RUSSIAN TEA

1   box instant lemon tea mix
2   cups Tang
2½   cups sugar
1½   teaspoons ground cinnamon
1   teaspoon ground cloves

> Mix all ingredients together well. Add 2 teaspoons mix to 1 cup hot water per serving.

JELLO PUNCH

4   cups boiling water
2½ cups sugar
2   6 ounce cans frozen orange juice
3   3 ounce packages Jello, your favorite
8   cups cold water
2   6 ounce cans frozen lemonade
1   48 ounce can pineapple juice
1   1-liter bottle gingerale

> Add hot water to Jello and dissolve. Add cold water and other juices. Add water according to directions on juice cans. Add gingerale just before serving. If using lime Jello, float lime sherbet in punch bowl, etc.

OLD FASHIONED STRAWBERRY SODA

1   10 ounce package frozen strawberries in syrup, thawed
3   cups strawberry ice cream, divided
2   12 ounce cans cream soda, divided
whipped cream
4   whole strawberries

> Mash thawed strawberries with a fork until they are well blended with their own syrup. Add 1 cup ice cream and ½ cup cream soda: stir well. Spoon an equal amount of strawberries mixture into 4 - 14 ounce soda glasses, top with remaining ice cream, and fill glasses with remaining cream soda. Garnish each glass with a dollop of whipped cream and a strawberry. Yields: 4 servings.

PEACH FUZZ

6   medium peaches, peeled and quartered
1   cup sugar
⅓   bottle one fifth vodka or rum
1   6 ounce can frozen undiluted lemonade or limeade

> Put all ingredients in blender till just mixed. Pour out ½ of mixture for later and add crushed ice to remaining ½, blend till mushy stage. Pour into glasses and serve.

QUICK AND EASY PUNCH

5   12 ounce cans Fresca
Color as desired with food coloring
1   46 ounce can pineapple juice

> Mix together: pour over ice ring in punch bowl.

SWEET SOUTHERN TEA

3   family size Tetley tea bags (or 6 regular tea bags)
1¾ cup sugar

> Bring 1 quart water to a rolling boil. Add the tea bags. Remove from heat and let sit 5 - 10 minutes. Put sugar into a gallon container and pour the steeped tea over the sugar. Finish filling gallon container with water and stir.

TEA PUNCH

2   quarts sweet tea
3   cans frozen orange juice
2   cans frozen lemonade
1   48 ounce can pineapple juice
2   quarts gingerale

> Mix orange juice and lemonade according to directions on cans. Mix together with tea. Add gingerale just before serving.

SOUPS
and
SALADS

Index

AMBROSIA CREAM CHEESE MOLD

1   envelope unflavored gelatin
½   cup cold water
1   15 ounce can pineapple chunks and juice
⅓   cup sugar
juice of 1 lemon
2   3 ounce packages cream cheese, softened
1   orange, peeled, sectioned and diced
½   cup chopped pecans, optional
½   cup flaked coconut

Soften gelatin in cold water and let stand 5 minutes. Drain pineapple and reserve juice. Add enough water to juice to make 1 cup. Place juice in 2 quart saucepan. Heat to boiling, add gelatin mixture and stir until dissolved. Remove from heat and stir in sugar, lemon juice and cream cheese. Blend well. Chill until gelatin is partially set. Fold in pineapple chunks, orange, pecans and coconut. Spoon into a lightly greased 1 quart mold. Chill until firm.

APRICOT SALAD

1   3 ounce package apricot or orange Jello
1   cup hot water
1   15 ounce can crushed pineapple
1   8 ounce carton sour cream
1   15 ounce can apricots, drained and chopped

Dissolve Jello in hot water. Let chill slightly and fold in other ingredients.

BLUEBERRY AMBROSIA

1   cup crushed pineapple or pineapple chunks, drained
1   15 ounce can fruit cocktail, drained
1   15 ounce can blueberries, drained
2   cups miniature marshmallows
1   cup sour cream
3   tablespoons powdered sugar

Mix all ingredients, cover and let stand in refrigerator at least 1 hour before serving.

BLUEBERRY SALAD

1   6 ounce package raspberry Jello
2   cups hot water
1   15 ounce can blueberries, undrained
1   15 ounce can crushed pineapple, reserve
4   tablespoons juice for topping

Dissolve Jello in hot water. Add blueberries and pineapple, place in refrigerator to congeal.

TOPPING

1   8 ounce package cream cheese
1   8 ounce carton sour cream
½   cup sugar
½   cup pecans, optional
4   tablespoons pineapple juice

Blend cream cheese, sour cream, pineapple juice, and sugar well. Add nuts if desired. Spread over top of salad after it congeals.

BROCCOLI SALAD

1-2 heads broccoli

8   slices cooked bacon

5   green onions, chopped

½   cup raisins

1   cup mayonnaise

2   tablespoons apple cider vinegar

¼   cup sugar

> Cut heads of broccoli into bite size pieces. Add bacon, onions, and raisins. Mix together mayonnaise, vinegar and sugar. Toss over salad. Refrigerate several hours. Serve.

BRUNSWICK STEW

5   pounds Boston Butt pork roast

6   medium onions, chopped

8   cans diced tomatoes

4   cans English peas

2   12 ounce cans tomato sauce

4   cups ketchup

1   20 ounce bottle Worcestershire sauce

lemon juice

4   cans cream style corn

salt and pepper to taste

> Cook meat in slow cooker. Shred and add remaining ingredients. Simmer 1 hour.

BRUNSWICK STEW - SUPREME

3   cups cooked chicken, chopped
1½   pounds coarsely ground chuck beef
½   pound coarsely ground lean pork
1   large onion, chopped
1   29 ounce bottle ketchup
2   15 ounce cans tomatoes, diced
2   15 ounce cans cream style corn

> Cook beef, pork and onion in 1 cup chicken stock with enough water added to cover for 1 hour. Add salt to taste. Add ketchup and tomatoes and cook another hour. Add corn, chicken and 1 teaspoon red pepper. Cook slowly 1 hour.

BUTTERMILK SALAD

1   8 ounce carton Cool Whip
1   6 ounce package Jello, strawberry or your favorite flavor
1   10 ounce package frozen strawberries, if using strawberry
2   cups buttermilk
1   cup hot water
1   15 ounce can crushed pineapple, undrained

> Mix together Jello, hot water, pineapple, buttermilk, and fruit. Put in refrigerator to thicken slightly. Then stir in 1 8 ounce carton of Cool Whip and return to refrigerator to congeal.

CAULIFLOWER BROCCOLI SALAD

1	head cauliflower	1	3 ounce jar real bacon bits
1	bunch broccoli	1	cup sour cream
1	10 ounce package frozen green peas, thawed	1	cup mayonnaise
1	package buttermilk dressing mix	1	cup sharp Cheddar cheese, shredded
		1	8 ounce can sliced water chestnuts

Cut cauliflower and broccoli into bite size pieces. Combine cauliflower, broccoli, peas, cheese, water chestnuts, and bacon bits in large bowl. Set aside. Mix sour cream, mayonnaise and dressing, pour over vegetables. Chill. Yields: 8 -10 servings.

CHEESY CHICKEN SOUP

4	cups chicken broth	⅓	cup all purpose flour
1½	cups diced potatoes	3	cups milk
1	cup diced celery	1	tablespoon soy sauce
1	cup diced carrots	1	16 ounce loaf Velveeta
½	cup diced onions	2	cups chopped cooked chicken
2	tablespoons butter		

Combine first five ingredients in large saucepan: cover and cook five minutes. Melt butter in Dutch oven over low heat. Add flour and stir until smooth. Add milk, cook one minute, stirring constantly until thickened and bubbly. Gradually stir in vegetable mixture, soy sauce, cheese and chicken. Cook until cheese melts and soup is piping hot. Yields: two and a half quarts. You can add additional vegetables or cheese and season with a dash of cayenne pepper or Tabasco.

CHERRY SALAD

2   3 ounce packages cherry Jello
2   cups boiling water
2   cups miniature marshmallows
1   8 ounce package cream cheese, softened
1   large can, crushed pineapple, undrained
1   cup chopped pecans, optional
2   cups whipping cream, whipped

Dissolve Jello in boiling water, add marshmallows and stir until almost dissolved. Add softened cream cheese and blend until smooth. Add pineapple and nuts. Fold in whipping cream. Place in refrigerator and congeal.

CHICKEN SALAD

6   chicken breasts
5   boiled eggs
¼   cup dill relish
Kraft mayonnaise

Boil chicken in salted water until tender, then shred. Add chopped boiled eggs, dill relish, and enough mayonnaise to make good consistency. Add black pepper to taste. May add green seedless grapes and chopped nuts for variation.

CHINESE CHICKEN SALAD

3   chicken breasts
1   small can chow mein noodles
3   green onions, chopped
1   4 ounce package sliced almonds or roasted peanuts
¼   cup sesame seeds, optional
1   head lettuce
1   small can bean sprouts
water chestnuts, optional

Cube or shred cooked chicken. Combine all ingredients. Just before serving, prepare dressing.

DRESSING

6   tablespoons sugar
4   tablespoons vinegar
2   teaspoons salt
¼   cup salad oil
¼   teaspoon pepper
juice of 1 lemon

Mix together all ingredients and serve over salad.

CLASSIC CHICKEN SALAD

3   cups cooked chicken, diced
1½ cups celery, finely chopped
½   cup pecans, finely chopped
3   tablespoons Durkees Sandwich & Salad Sauce
juice of ½ lemon
salt and pepper to taste

Mix all ingredients. Toss lightly with enough mayonnaise to moisten.

COCA COLA SALAD

1 can dark pitted cherries
1 15 ounce can crushed pineapple
1 6 ounce package cherry Jello
1 cup chopped pecans
1 8 ounce package cream cheese
1 16 ounce can Coke

Soften Jello in cold water, let stand 5 minutes. Drain pineapple and reserve juice; add enough water to juice to make 1 cup. Place juice in 2 quart saucepan, heat to boiling, add gelatin mixture and stir until dissolved. Remove from heat. Stir in sugar, lemon juice and cream cheese. Blend well. Chill until gelatin is partially set. Fold in pineapple chunks, orange, pecans and coconut. Spoon into a lightly greased 1 quart mold, chill until firm. Cut cherries in pieces. Take juice from cherries and pineapple, about 2 cups, and bring to a boil. Add Jello and stir until dissolved. Add cream cheese and mix until dissolved. Fold in rest of ingredients. Add Coke and mold.

DRESSING

10-12 large marshmallows
1 cup sour cream
10 Maraschino cherries

Mix in blender and use cherry juice for coloring. Serve over Coca Cola Salad.

COMPOTE FRUIT SALAD

2   cups fresh strawberries or 1 box frozen

3   fresh oranges, peeled and sliced

1   15 ounce can chunk pineapple, drained

2   medium bananas, peeled and sliced

1   15 ounce can fruit cocktail, drained

orange juice

>   Mix fruit together and cover with orange juice. Chill and serve.

CRABAPPLE SALAD

1   jar crabapples

1   3 ounce package lemon Jello

1   3 ounce package strawberry Jello

1   15 ounce can crushed pineapple

½   cup celery, chopped

½   cup chopped nuts.

>   Drain juice off crabapples and add to the juice enough water to make 2 cups. Heat to near boiling. Pour over both jellos and stir until dissolved. Add 2 cups ice water and chill until firm enough to hold up fruit. Add other ingredients. Note: mash up crabapples after getting out seed.

CREAM OF MUSHROOM SOUP

3   tablespoons butter
2   tablespoons olive oil
¾   cup finely chopped shallots
2   pounds white cultivated mushrooms, thinly sliced
⅓   cup cream Sherry
1   teaspoon fresh thyme leaves
salt and freshly ground black pepper
3   tablespoons all purpose flour
3½ cups low salt chicken broth, reserving ½ cup
½   cup milk or heavy cream
¼   teaspoon nutmeg
½   cup sour cream, may omit

In a large saucepan melt butter with the olive oil over moderate heat. Add the shallots and cook until tender, about 2 - 3 minutes. Add the sliced mushrooms, thyme leaves, salt and pepper cooking until all of the liquid rendered from the mushrooms evaporates. Add the Sherry and cook until evaporated. Remove a ½ cup of the cooked mushrooms and reserve. Stir in the flour and cook for 2 - 3 minutes. Add 3 cups of the chicken broth, bring to a simmer and cook for 15 minutes. In a blender, puree the soup in batches until smooth. For a very smooth soup pass through a sieve. Return soup to saucepan, bring to a simmer and whisk in cream. Add reserved chicken broth to achieve desired consistency. Adjust seasoning with salt, pepper and nutmeg. Lower heat and whisk in sour cream if desired. Keep soup warm but do not simmer or boil. Serve soup garnished with reserved cooked mushrooms.

CREAM OF PIMENTO SOUP

1   4 ounce jar diced pimento, undrained
2   tablespoons grated onion
3   tablespoons butter
½   tablespoon salt
3   tablespoons all purpose flour
¼   tablespoon hot sauce
1   14 ounce can chicken broth
1   ½ cup half and half
sour cream for garnish

Process pimento in blender until smooth. Set aside. Melt butter over low heat: add flour: stirring until smooth. Cook, stirring constantly, about 1 minute. Gradually add broth and half and half to saucepan. Cook over medium heat, stirring constantly until thickened and bubbly. Stir in pimento, onion, salt and hot sauce. Cook over medium low heat stirring constantly, until heated. Yields: 3 ½ cups.

CREAM OF POTATO SOUP

5   baking potatoes, peel and cube
1   small onion, chopped fine
5   cubes chicken bullion

Place all ingredients in a large pot, cover with water. Cook until tender.

PART 2
1   stick butter
1   8 ounce cup sour cream
1   pound Velveeta cheese, cubed

Add all ingredients to cooked potatoes. Stir until blended well and serve.

CUCUMBER SALAD

2   cucumbers, unpeeled, grated
1   medium onion, grated
2   3 ounce packages lemon Jello
1   cup hot water
2   teaspoons vinegar
⅔   cup mayonnaise
½   cup sour cream
1   12 ounce carton cottage cheese

> Squeeze cucumbers and onions in towel until dry. Dissolve Jello in hot water. Add all ingredients: mix well. Pour into mold. Place in refrigerator to congeal.

CURRIED FRUIT

1   29 ounce can pear halves
1   29 ounce can peach halves
1   15 ounce can pineapple chunks
½   cup Maraschino cherries
⅓   cup butter
¾   cup brown sugar
1   tablespoon curry powder

> Drain fruit. Place in casserole. Melt butter, sugar and curry. Mix well: pour over fruit. Bake, covered for 1 hour at 325 degrees.

DELIGHTFUL FRUIT SALAD

1	can pineapple chunks
2	apples, red or green, diced
½	bag miniature marshmallows
½	cup shredded coconut
½	cup raisins
1	cup sour cream
½	cup powdered sugar

Mix sour cream and powdered sugar. Toss over fruit. Chill and serve.

DEVILED EGGS

6   hard boiled eggs, cut lengthwise
Thousand Island dressing
salt and pepper to taste

Mash yolks and mix with Thousand Island dressing as needed. Season with salt and pepper. Stuff into egg whites.

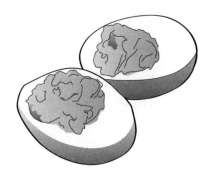

EASY FRUIT SALAD

1   3 ounce package lime Jello
1   12 ounce carton Cool Whip
1   8 ounce carton cottage cheese
1   15 ounce can fruit cocktail, drained
1   small crushed pineapple, drained
1   cup nuts, optional

> Mix dry Jello with Cool Whip and add cottage cheese, fruits and nuts. Chill and serve. Note: this is also very good with strawberry Jello and fresh strawberries.

ENGLISH PEA SALAD

1   15 ounce can Le Seur English peas
½   cup diced sweet pickles
2   hard boiled eggs, chopped
½   cup chopped pimento

> Drain peas, pickles and pimento. Place in salad bowl and add chopped eggs. Toss with enough mayonnaise to coat evenly. Season with salt and pepper. Chill and serve on lettuce.

FRESH FRUIT SALAD

3   cups orange juice
1   cup pineapple juice
assortment of fruit: bananas, kiwi, grapes, pineapple, apples
1   cup sugar

> Mix juices and sugar. Pour over fresh fruit and serve.

FRESH FRUIT SALAD WITH POPPY SEED DRESSING

1   cantaloupe
1   pound seedless green grapes, halved
2   bananas
2   apples, diced
1   11 ounce can pineapple tidbits, drained
1   11 ounce can mandarin orange sections, drained

> With a melon scoop, shape cantaloupe into balls. Gently combine fruits and use the sauce below for a dressing.

POPPY SEED DRESSING

¾   cup sugar
1   teaspoon salt
1   teaspoon paprika
¼   cup orange juice
2½   tablespoons lemon juice
1   cup salad oil
1   teaspoon grated onion
1   tablespoon poppy seeds

> Mix all ingredients together. Toss over fruit.

FRESH TOMATO DRESSING

1   cup olive oil
½   cup balsamic vinegar
1   tablespoon garlic powder
1   tablespoon sugar
1   tablespoon salt
1   teaspoon pepper
1   tablespoon thyme, ground
3   large tomatoes, peeled and chopped

Whisk together oil, vinegar, garlic powder, sugar, salt, pepper, and thyme. Peel and chop tomato to about ½ inch pieces. Stir tomatoes into mixture. Cover and let stand at room temperature 1 hour, stirring occasionally. Cover and chill 8 hours. Yields: 4 cups. Note: dressing may be stored in refrigerator up to 1 month. Stir additional fresh chopped tomato into dressing after each use.

FROZEN CHERRY SALAD

1   can cherry pie filling
1   can sweetened condensed milk
4-6 teaspoons lemon juice
1   can crushed pineapple
1   16 ounce carton Cool Whip

Mix cherry pie filling, condensed milk, lemon juice and crushed pineapple. Fold in Cool Whip. Freeze 24 hours covered.

FROZEN CRANBERRY SALAD

2   3 ounce packages cream cheese
2   tablespoons sugar
2   tablespoons mayonnaise
1   can whole berry cranberry sauce
½   cup chopped nuts
½   pint whipping cream or Cool Whip
1   cup crushed pineapple, drained

> Combine cheese, sugar and mayonnaise. Add pineapple, cranberry sauce and pecans. Fold in cream. Freeze. Can be frozen in individual containers, then removed. After frozen, place in plastic bag until served.

FRUIT SALAD SUPREME

2   cans mandarin oranges
1   can pineapple tidbits
1   cup miniature marshmallows
1   can Eagle Brand milk
½   cup lemon juice

> Mix the Eagle Brand milk and lemon juice, toss on fruit and marshmallows. Serve.

GERMAN POTATO SALAD

6-8 medium potatoes
1   medium onion, chopped
1   bottle Italian dressing
ground black pepper
celery seed

> Boil potatoes in salted water until tender; drain. Mix other ingredients together and toss over potatoes. Cover and refrigerate.

GRAPE SALAD

1   8 ounce carton cream cheese, softened
1   8 ounce carton sour cream
1   8 ounce carton Cool Whip
½   cup sugar
1   teaspoon vanilla
2   pounds red seedless grapes
2   pounds green seedless grapes
½   cup light brown sugar
½   cup chopped pecans

> Mix together cream cheese, sour cream, Cool Whip, sugar and vanilla. Wash and dry grapes very well. Mix with the cream mixture. Pour into a 9 x 13 inch dish. Top with brown sugar and chopped pecans.

HAPPY DAY FRUIT SALAD

1   4 ounce package instant vanilla pudding mix
1   cup whipping cream, whipped
1   29 ounce can fruit cocktail, drained
1   11 ounce can mandarin orange sections, drained
1   4 ounce jar Maraschino cherries, drained and halved
4   bananas diced
1   cup miniature marshmallows

Prepare pudding according to directions on package, fold in whipped cream. Fold in remaining ingredients and chill well.

HOLIDAY SALAD

4   3 ounce packages cream cheese
1   pint whipping cream
½   cup sugar
4   teaspoons mayonnaise
2   cans mandarin orange slices
1   cup pecans
1   cup red cherries
1   cup green cherries
2   cans pineapple tidbits

Drain all fruit, very well, this is very important. Cut fruit if desired. Whip cream, then add to beaten cream cheese and sugar. Beat until smooth. Add mayonnaise, fruit and pecans. Refrigerate until ready to serve.

HONEY DRESSING FOR SPINACH

1   cup sugar

½   cup honey

2   tablespoons ground ginger

⅓   cup lime juice

⅓   cup water

2   cups corn oil

2   tablespoons dry mustard

Mix together well and serve over Spinach Salad, page 53.

LIME DELIGHT

1   6 ounce package lime Jello

2   cups boiling water

2   cups miniature marshmallows

1   8 ounce package cream cheese, softened

1   15 ounce can crushed pineapple

1   cup chopped pecans, optional

1   16 ounce carton whipping cream, whipped

Dissolve Jello in boiling water; add marshmallows and stir until mostly dissolved. Add softened cream cheese and blend until smooth. Add pineapple and nuts and fold in whipping cream.

LUSCIOUS PEAR SALAD

1   29 ounce can pears, sliced
juice from pears
10 Maraschino cherries, halves
1   8 ounce cream cheese
1   3 ounce package orange Jello
1   12 ounce package Cool Whip

> Boil juice from pears; put hot juice in blender. Add cream cheese and Jello and blend well. Add Cool Whip to blender; blend well. Place sliced pears and cherries in bottom of mold; pour blender mixture over pears. Chill until firm.

MANDARIN - ORANGE MOLD

2   11 ounce cans mandarin orange sections, drained
2   3 ounce packages orange Jello
1   cup boiling water
1   15 ounce can crushed pineapple, undrained
1   16 ounce carton orange sherbet, softened
1   16 ounce carton whipping cream, whipped

> Dissolve Jello in boiling water. Set aside to cool but not in refrigerator. Add orange sections and pineapple; then add sherbet and fold in whipping cream.

MARINATED COLESLAW

1   large cabbage, shredded
2   medium bell peppers, finely chopped
3   medium onions, finely chopped
1⅓ cups vinegar
2½ cups sugar
⅔   cup water
1½ teaspoons mustard seeds
1   teaspoon celery seeds
½   teaspoon turmeric
1½ teaspoons salt

> Combine cabbage, green pepper and onion in a large bowl: set aside. Combine remaining ingredients in a medium saucepan, mixing well. Bring to a boil: immediately pour over vegetables. Cover and chill 12 hours, stirring occasionally.

MARINATED VEGETABLE SALAD

1   15 ounce can Le-Seur English peas
1   15 ounce can French style green beans
1   15 ounce can bean sprouts
1   2 ounce jar chopped pimento
1   8 ounce jar sliced water chestnuts
1   5 ounce jar green olives, sliced
1   medium bell pepper, chopped
½   cup celery, diced
1   small onion, sliced in rings

> Drain vegetables and mix together.

MARINADE

1   cup white vinegar
1   cup water
½   cup salad oil
½   cup sugar

> Mix together until sugar is dissolved. Pour over vegetables. Cover and marinate overnight in refrigerator. Drain and serve.

ORANGE - CARROT SALAD

1   6 ounce package orange Jello
2   cups boiling water
1½ cups cold water
2   large carrots, shredded
1   11 ounce can mandarin oranges, drained
1   15 ounce can crushed pineapple, undrained
½   cup chopped pecans

> Dissolve Jello in boiling water and stir in cold water. Chill until partially set. Fold carrots, oranges, pineapple and chopped pecans into thickened Jello. Spoon into an oiled 2 quart mold: chill until set. Unmold onto a bed of lettuce and garnish with carrot curls and pecan halves.

ORANGE SALAD

1   3 ounce package orange Jello
1   cup hot water
1   8 ounce package softened cream cheese
1   small jar of maraschino cherries
1   15 ounce can crushed pineapple
1   12 ounce carton Cool Whip

> Mix first three ingredients together until smooth. Place in refrigerator to cool, do not let thicken. Add ½ cup chopped Maraschino cherries and crushed pineapple. Whip in Cool Whip. Put in refrigerator to congeal.

PEACH ASPIC

1   envelope plain gelatin
2   3 ounce packages peach flavored Jello
1½ cups boiling water
1   cup orange juice
3   tablespoons lemon juice
2   cups fresh mashed peaches, sweetened to taste

> Dissolve both gelatins in boiling water: add orange juice and lemon juice. Add peaches. Pour into mold and congeal. Serve with dressing of cream cheese and mayonnaise.

PICKLED PEACH SALAD

2   3 ounce packages lemon Jello
1   cup boiling water
2   cups cold water
3   fresh oranges, sliced
1   jar peach pickles, chopped and juice
1   cup chopped nuts
1   small jar cherries, chopped

> Dissolve Jello in boiling water. Add 2 cups of cold water and the peach juice. Stir in nuts and fruits. Congeal.

POTATO SALAD DIVINE

2½ pounds potatoes
1   cup Kraft mayonnaise
1   cup sour cream
3   tablespoons chives, frozen or dried
chopped onions, optional

Cut potatoes into cubes. Boil in salted water until tender. Drain well. Mix mayonnaise, sour cream and chives together. Toss over potatoes. Chill and serve.

RAW VEGETABLE SALAD

1   medium cauliflower, separated
1   small package radishes, chopped
1   bunch fresh spring onions, chopped use the tops too
1   cup cucumbers, sliced
1   cup yellow squash
1   bunch fresh broccoli, separated and cut
1   cup mayonnaise
1   8 ounce carton sour cream
1   package Good Seasons Garlic Cheese Mix
1   tablespoon sesame seed

Mix mayonnaise, sour cream, garlic cheese mix and sesame seed together, toss over vegetables. Refrigerate several hours before serving.

RICE SALAD

1   cup rice, cook until tender, rinse and cool
1   cup celery
1   small onion, grated
¾   cup chopped stuffed green olives
1   8 ounce carton sour cream
1   teaspoon vinegar
½   cup mayonnaise

> To cooled rice add celery, olives and onions. Mix sour cream, vinegar and mayonnaise. Add to other ingredients and mix well,. Let stand several hours or overnight.

SIMPLY "LUSCIOUS" SALAD

1   can crushed pineapple, drained
1½ cups sugar
1   cup sour cream
2   16 ounce cartons Cool Whip
1   cup chopped nuts

> Mix together well. Chill and serve.

SPINACH SALAD/MANDARIN ORANGE

spinach leaves, chopped
mandarin orange slices
bean sprouts
almonds

> Mix together and serve with Poppy Seed dressing, page 41 or Honey Dressing, page 46.

SPINACH SALAD/RASPBERRY

spinach leaves, chopped
raspberries, fresh
almonds
bean sprouts

Mix together and serve with raspberry dressing.

STRAWBERRY SALAD

1   6 ounce package strawberry Jello
1   cup boiling water
2   10 ounce packages frozen sliced strawberries, thawed
1   15 ounce can crushed pineapple
2   medium bananas, mashed
1   cup chopped nuts, optional
1   16 ounce carton sour cream

Dissolve Jello in boiling water, add strawberries, pineapple, bananas, and nuts. Stir in sour cream, mix well. Pour into mold and congeal.

TACO SOUP

1   pound lean ground beef
1   large onion, chopped
3   16 ounce cans Mexican style chili beans, undrained
1   16 ounce can whole kernel corn, undrained
1   16 ounce can chopped tomatoes, undrained
1   15 ounce can tomato sauce
1½ cups water
1   4 ounce can chopped green chilies
1   package taco seasoning mix
1   envelope Ranch style salad dressing mix

> Cook ground beef and onion in a large Dutch oven over medium high heat until meat is browned, stirring until it crumbles: drain. Stir in beans and next 7 ingredients. Bring to a boil: reduce heat, and simmer, uncovered 15 minutes. Serve with desired toppings. Yields: 3 ½ quarts.

Toppings

tortilla chips
shredded cheese
shredded lettuce
chopped tomatoes
sour cream

TACO SOUP - FAVORITE

1   can stewed tomatoes

3   cans water

3   16 ounce cans minestrone soup or 3 small cans & 3 cans water

4   boneless chicken breasts, cooked and shredded

1   can rotel chili tomatoes and green chilies

1   can chili beans

1   tablespoon chili powder

salt to taste

> Put all ingredients in heavy saucepan, bring to a boil. Let simmer 30 minutes. Great with Fritos. You may substitute 1 ½ lb ground chuck for chicken.

TAILGATE SALAD

1   head lettuce, shredded

1   cup celery, chopped

1   cup onions, chopped

1   medium bell pepper, chopped

1   can Le Seur English peas, drained

1   cup Miracle Whip

2   teaspoons sugar, sprinkled over

1   cup Cheddar cheese, grated

1   cup bacon, cooked and crumbled

> Put by layers in order given into casserole. Cover and refrigerate overnight.

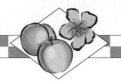

TANGY TOMATO ASPIC

1¼ cups boiling water
1   3 ounce package lemon flavored Jello
1   package Knox gelatin
1   8 ounce can tomato sauce
1½ tablespoons vinegar
½   teaspoon salt
½   teaspoon onion juice
⅛   teaspoon red pepper sauce
dash ground cloves
2   cups celery diced

> Mix the gelatins together. Pour boiling water over gelatins in bowl, stirring until gelatin is dissolved. Stir in tomato sauce, vinegar and seasonings. Chill until slightly thickened but not set. Stir in celery. Pour into a 4 cup ring mold. Chill until firm. Just before serving, fill center of mold ring with your favorite seafood salad.

WINTER SOUP

¾   pound ground beef
¾   pound sausage
1   large onion, chopped
2   cans green beans, drained
2   cans diced tomatoes
4   cups water with 4 beef bullions
1   bay leaf
3   tablespoons Worcestershire sauce
1   cup red wine
salt and pepper to taste
½   teaspoon thyme
1   tablespoon dried parsley
⅓   cup brown rice or diced potatoes

Brown beef and sausage in a heavy saucepan. Drain. Saute the onion. Add all ingredients back into heavy saucepan. Cook until rice or potatoes are done.

YUMMY FRUIT SALAD

1   cup coconut
1   15 ounce can chunk pineapple, drained
1   15 ounce can fruit cocktail, drained
1   can mandarin orange slices, drained
1   cup miniature marshmallows
1   cup chopped nuts, optional
1   8 ounce carton sour cream

Combine all ingredients. Chill several hours before serving.

VEGETABLES
and
SIDE DISHES

Index

ASPARAGUS CASSEROLE

1   15 ounce can asparagus
½   box cheese Ritz crackers
4   tablespoons margarine
1   can cream of mushroom soup
1   teaspoon Worcestershire sauce
¼   teaspoon Tabasco
1   tablespoon chopped bell pepper
1   tablespoon chopped pimento
1   tablespoon grated onion

Mix all ingredients except crackers and margarine. Place layer of asparagus mixture in greased casserole dish. Layer half of crushed crackers, another layer of asparagus and remainder of cracker crumbs. Top with melted butter. Bake at 350 degrees for 30 minutes.

ASPARAGUS SUPREME

2   cans asparagus spears, drained
1   jar chopped pimentos
3   boiled eggs
8   slices American cheese
1   can cream of mushroom soup
Ritz cracker crumbs
¼   cup butter, melted

Place 1 can of asparagus in baking dish. Spread pimentos over asparagus. Place 1 ½ boiled eggs sliced over pimentos. Put 4 slices of cheese over top. Repeat layers. Top with cream of mushroom soup. Then top with Ritz cracker crumbs and the melted butter. Bake at 350 degrees until bubbly and brown on top, 20 - 25 minutes.

BAKED APPLES

6   large baking apples, peeled and cored
6   tablespoons sugar
1½   teaspoons ground cinnamon
1½   teaspoons ground nutmeg
2   tablespoons butter
½-¾ cup apple juice
red food coloring, optional

> Place apples in a shallow 2 quart casserole. Pour 1 tablespoon sugar into cavity of each apple. Sprinkle each with ¼ teaspoon cinnamon and ¼ teaspoon nutmeg, top with 1 teaspoon butter. Heat apple juice to boiling and add red food coloring if desired. Pour juice into casserole dish. Bake apples, uncovered, at 350 degrees for 50 - 60 minutes or until tender, basting occasionally with juice.

BAKED BEANS

5   15 ounce cans pork and beans
½   cup ketchup
½   cup hickory barbecue sauce
¼   cup mustard
⅓   cup Worcestershire sauce
¼   cup maple syrup
4-6 strips bacon

> Preheat oven to 425 degrees. Mix all ingredients, except bacon, with beans. Place in a 4 quart casserole. Place bacon on top. Bake for 75 minutes at 425 degrees.

BAKED BEANS MADE SIMPLE

1   24 ounce can pork and beans
¾   cup light brown sugar
1   cup ketchup
1   large onion, chopped
1   tablespoon prepared mustard
2-3 slices bacon

Mix together well. Lay bacon slices on top. Bake at 350 degrees 1 ½ - 2 hours.

BAKED SQUASH

3   pounds yellow summer squash
½   cup onions, chopped
½   cup bread crumbs
½   teaspoon black pepper
2   eggs
1   stick butter
1   tablespoon sugar
1   teaspoon salt

Wash and slice squash. Boil until tender; drain thoroughly, then mash. Add all ingredients except ½ of butter to squash. Melt remaining butter. Pour mixture in dish, then spread melted butter over top and sprinkle with bread crumbs. Bake at 375 degrees for 1 hour or until brown on top.

BEAN CASSEROLE

2   15 ounce cans French style green beans, drained
1   8 ounce can sliced mushrooms
1   15 ounce can bean sprouts
1   8 ounce can water chestnuts, drained
1   2 ounce jar chopped pimentos
2   cups grated sharp cheese
1   small onion, grated
1   can cream of mushroom soup
1   can cream of chicken soup
1   can French fried onion rings

Mix all ingredients together except soups and French Fried onion rings. Place mixture in casserole dish in layers with soups (mixed together) between layers and on top. Bake at 350 degrees for 30 minutes. Top with French fried onions and continue baking 15 more minutes. Yields 10-12 servings.

BROCCOLI

1   package family size frozen broccoli florets
1   stick butter, melted
1   teaspoon basil
1   teaspoon garlic salt
½   teaspoon salt

Place butter, basil, garlic salt, and salt in bottom of casserole dish. Place frozen broccoli on top. Cook in microwave 15 - 20 minutes or until tender.

BROCCOLI AND RICE CASSEROLE

1   large onion, chopped
1   medium bell pepper, chopped
6   stalks celery, chopped
1   medium jar Cheese Whiz
2   cans cream of mushroom soup
2   packages chopped broccoli in cheese sauce
1   cup white rice
1   stick butter
cheese for topping

> Sauté onions, bell pepper, celery, and broccoli in butter. Cook rice according to directions and mix Cheese Whiz with rice while hot. Mix all together and put in casserole and grate cheese on top. Bake at 350 degrees until bubbly.

BROCCOLI SOUFFLE

2   packages frozen chopped broccoli, cooked & chopped fine
1   cup mayonnaise
1   cup Cheddar cheese, grated
1   can cream of mushroom soup
½   teaspoon salt
4   eggs, well-beaten

> Mix all ingredients, add beaten eggs last. Spoon in baking dish and place dish in pan of water. Bake at 350 degrees for 45 minutes to 1 hour or when knife inserted comes out clean.

BROCCOLI CORN CASSEROLE

1   10 ounce package frozen chopped broccoli thawed until
    all liquid is out
¼   cup cracker crumbs
1   egg, well beaten
2   tablespoons butter, melted
1   tablespoon flaked onion
1   teaspoon salt
dash black pepper
1   1-pound can cream corn
¼   cup cracker crumbs
2   tablespoons butter, melted

Combine broccoli, corn, ¼ cup cracker crumbs, egg, butter, onion, salt, and pepper. Pour into a greased casserole dish. Blend
the remaining ¼ cup cracker crumbs and butter, sprinkle on
top. Cook at 350 degrees in uncovered casserole dish for 30 - 45
minutes.

CABBAGE CASSEROLE

2   cans crescent rolls
1½ pounds ground beef
1   small head cabbage
½   medium onion, chopped
1   can cream of mushroom soup
2   cups shredded Cheddar cheese

Unroll one can of crescent rolls and press in bottom of a greased 9 x 13 inch pan. Brown hamburger and onion; drain. Add cabbage, sliced thin, and add soup. Cook until cabbage is tender. Season with salt and pepper. Place this mixture over rolls in pan and then top with cheese. Unroll the second can of crescent rolls and place on top. Bake at 350 degrees for 30 minutes or until brown.

CANDIED TOMATOES

1   1 pound can tomatoes
1   cup sugar
2   tablespoons butter
¼   teaspoon pepper

Mix together, bring to a boil, reduce heat to simmer and cook until thick. This is delicious with vegetables.

CARROT CASSEROLE

12	medium carrots, sliced	¼	cup butter
1	small onion, minced	¼	cup flour
1	teaspoon salt	¼	teaspoon dry mustard
2	cups milk	½	teaspoon pepper
¼	teaspoon celery salt	1½	pounds grated cheese
3	cups buttered bread crumbs		

Preheat oven to 350 degrees. Cook carrots until tender; drain. In saucepan, melt butter, add onions, stir in flour, salt and mustard. Add milk and cook until smooth. Add pepper and celery salt. Place ⅓ carrots in buttered casserole dish. Add half of cheese; repeat layers. End with carrots on top. Pour sauce over carrots. Cover with bread crumbs. Bake 25 minutes at 350 degrees.

CAULIFLOWER WITH CHEESE SAUCE

1	medium cauliflower	4	tablespoons butter
4	tablespoons flour	2	cups milk
1½	cups grated Cheddar cheese	½	teaspoon salt

Cook cauliflower in boiling salted water until tender. Melt butter; stir in flour. Add milk gradually, stirring until thickened. Add cheese and salt. Place cauliflower in serving dish; cover with cheese sauce. Yields; 6-8 servings.

CHEDDAR BAKED POTATOES

1   can cream of mushroom soup

½   teaspoon paprika

½   teaspoon pepper

4   medium potatoes cut into ¼ inch slices

1   cup shredded Cheddar cheese

In small bowl combine soup, paprika, and pepper. In greased 2 quart oblong baking dish, arrange potatoes in overlapping rows. Sprinkle with cheese. Spoon soup mixture over cheese. Cover and bake at 400 degrees for 45 minutes. Uncover, bake 10 minutes longer or until potatoes are fork tender.

CHEESE GRITS

1½ cups regular grits

6   cups water

1   teaspoon salt

4   large eggs

½   cup butter

2   tablespoons seasoning salt

½   pound Velveeta cheese, grated

½   pound sharp Cheddar cheese, grated

dash Tabasco

Cook grits in boiling, salted water for 20 minutes. Remove from heat and add eggs, butter, seasoning salt, cheeses and Tabasco. Stir until all ingredients are melted and blended. Pour into a 3 quart buttered casserole dish and bake at 350 degrees for 40 minutes. This may be frozen before baking. Yields; 12-14 servings.

CHILI PEPPER RICE

1   cup uncooked rice
1   16 ounce carton sour cream
2   4 ounce cans green chili peppers, chopped
1   pound Monterey Jack cheese or Cheddar cheese
paprika
butter

> Cook rice as usual. Mix cooked rice with the sour cream. Spoon half the rice mixture into baking dish. Spread the chopped peppers over this. Cut the cheese in chunks and mash down all through the rice. Put remaining rice on top of this. Sprinkle with paprika, butter and shredded cheese. Bake at 350 degrees for 30 - 40 minutes.

COLE SLAW

1   cabbage, finely shredded
2   cups Kraft mayonnaise
¾   cup sugar
1   cup diced sweet pickles
salt and pepper to taste

> Mix all ingredients together and serve.

CRAN-APPLE CASSEROLE

3 cups unpeeled apples, sliced
2 cups raw cranberries
¾ cup sugar
1 stick butter
1 cup flour
½ cup brown sugar
½ cup chopped nuts

> Combine apples and cranberries in baking dish. Sprinkle with sugar. Melt butter and add flour, brown sugar and nuts. Spread over fruit. Bake at 350 degrees for 45 - 60 minutes. Great as a dessert. Serve with ice cream over top.

EGGPLANT CASSEROLE

1 large eggplant
1 cup milk
2 eggs, beaten
1 cup grated Cheddar cheese
1 cup Italian bread crumbs
1 tablespoon butter
½ teaspoon salt
½ teaspoon pepper
½ teaspoon oregano
2 large tomatoes, sliced

> Peel and cube eggplant. Cook in water until tender and drain well. Combine all ingredients, mix with eggplant. Pour into greased casserole dish and bake 40 minutes at 350 degrees.

ENGLISH PEA CASSEROLE

1	can cream of mushroom soup
1	8 ounce carton sour cream
1	teaspoon salt
¼	teaspoon garlic salt
4	15 ounce cans Leseur green peas
1	cup Ritz crackers, crushed
¼	pound grated Cheddar cheese
½	cup melted butter

Mix together mushroom soup, sour cream, salt, garlic salt and green peas, spoon into casserole dish. Cover with 1 cup Ritz crackers crumbs; sprinkle crumbs with ¼ pound grated cheese and drizzle with ½ cup melt butter. Cover and bake 20 - 30 minutes.

GREEN TOMATO CASSEROLE

4	medium green tomatoes, sliced
3	medium potatoes, sliced thin
1	medium Vidalia onion, sliced
5	tablespoons flour
¼	cup water

Slice tomatoes, potatoes and onions. Toss flour over vegetables and mix well. Add salt, pepper and garlic salt to taste. Place in casserole dish and pour ¼ cup water over top. Cover and bake at 350 degrees for 40 minutes or until potatoes are tender. Cover top with grated cheese and put back into oven to melt.

HARVARD BEETS

1   15 ounce can beets
¼   cup sugar
1   tablespoon cornstarch
¼   teaspoon salt
2   tablespoons vinegar
1   tablespoon butter

> Drain beets; reserve liquid. Combine sugar, cornstarch and salt in saucepan. Add vinegar and 2 tablespoons of beet liquid. Cook, stirring constantly, until thick and clear. Add beets and butter. If too thick add beet juice as desired.

MACARONI AND CHEESE

1   8 ounce box elbow macaroni
1½   pounds Cheddar cheese, grated
½   stick butter
3   tablespoons flour
3   cups milk

> Cook macaroni in salted, boiling water until tender; drain. In casserole dish place layer of grated cheese and layer of macaroni beginning and ending with cheese. Sprinkle with black pepper. Make white sauce by melting butter, stir in the flour until smooth. Add the milk and cook, stirring constantly until it begins to thicken. Pour over macaroni and cheese. Bake in 400 degree oven until brown and bubbly.

MARINATED CARROTS

2	pounds carrots	1	small bell pepper, sliced into rings
1	medium onion, sliced into rings	1	can tomato soup
½	cup salad oil	1	cup sugar
¾	cup vinegar	1	teaspoon prepared mustard
1	teaspoon Worcestershire sauce		salt and pepper

Slice and boil carrots in salted water until fork tender, cool. Alternate layers of carrots, bell pepper and onions in dish. Make marinade of remaining ingredients, beating until well blended. Pour mixture over vegetables and refrigerate. Will keep for several weeks.

MEXICAN MACARONI AND CHEESE

1 8 ounce package macaroni
1 15 ounce can Mexican style tomatoes, undrained and chopped
1 can cream of mushroom soup
1 8 ounce carton sour cream
1 5 ounce can chopped green chilies
1 cup shredded Monterey Jack cheese
1 cup shredded Cheddar cheese

Cook macaroni according to package directions and drain. Combine macaroni, tomatoes, and next 3 ingredients. Stir in half of cheese. Pour into a lightly greased 2 quart baking dish; top with remaining cheeses. Bake at 350 degrees for 30 minutes.

ORIENTAL COLE SLAW

1   package broccoli slaw

3   green onions, finely chopped

2   20 ounce packages slivered almonds, brown on cookie sheet
      at 350 degrees

2   packages uncooked Raman noodles-broken up, disregard the
      seasoning in the package

      Mix all ingredients together.

DRESSING

4½   tablespoons sugar

6½   tablespoons rice vinegar

½   cup olive oil

1½   teaspoons salt

1   teaspoon pepper

      Mix all ingredients together and chill. Pour and toss dressing
      over salad about 30 minutes before serving. This just lets the
      noodles soften and the salad takes on the flavor of the dressing.
      I don't recommend making it the day before.

PINEAPPLE CASSEROLE

2   cans pineapple tidbits
1   cup grated Cheddar cheese
1   8 ounce package cream cheese, softened
1   cup sugar
6   tablespoons pineapple juice
6   tablespoons flour
1½ sleeves Ritz crackers
1   stick butter

Drain pineapple, combine with Cheddar cheese; set aside. Combine cream cheese with sugar, pineapple juice and flour. Mix with pineapple Cheddar cheese mixture. Crush 1 ½ sleeves Ritz crackers and place on top. Melt butter and pour over cracker crumbs. Bake at 350 degrees for 20 minutes or until hot and bubbly.

POTATO – CHEESE CASSEROLE

6   medium sliced potatoes
2   cans cream of mushroom soup
2   cups milk
2   medium onions, thinly sliced
2   cups Cheddar cheese, grated
salt and pepper
paprika

Cook potatoes in salted water until tender. Combine soup and milk, stirring well. Layer half of potatoes, onion and cheese in a greased 2 quart casserole dish. Sprinkle with salt and pepper. Pour half of soup mixture over cheese. Repeat layers. Sprinkle paprika over top. Bake at 300 degrees for 45 minutes or until bubbly.

POTATO CASSEROLE

1	stick butter
½	cup onions
2	pounds frozen hash brown potatoes
1	can cream of chicken soup
2	cups grated Cheddar cheese
2	8 ounce cartons sour cream
1	teaspoon salt
¼	cup chopped pimento
½	stick butter, melted
2	cups cornflake crumbs

Melt margarine in skillet. Sauté onions. Add the next 7 ingredients. Mix well. Pour Into a 9 ½ x 13 ½ inch buttered casserole dish. Bake at 350 degrees for 1 hour. Mix the melted margarine and the cornflake crumbs and pat them into a crust over the potatoes during the last 10 minutes of baking.

POTATO SOUFFLE

6   medium baked sweet potatoes
1½ cups sugar
2   eggs
½   cup softened butter
½   cup milk
¼   teaspoon nutmeg
½   teaspoon cinnamon

Combine sweet potatoes, sugar, eggs, ½ cup butter, milk and spices in a mixing bowl. Beat well. Spoon into a lightly buttered 1 ½ quart baking dish. Bake at 300 degrees for 30 minutes.

Topping

½   cup butter
½   cup firmly packed brown sugar
½   cup chopped pecans
¾   cup cornflake crumbs

Melt butter and brown sugar in a saucepan. Add nuts and cornflake crumbs. Spread over potato mixture. Bake 15 minutes longer.

REGENCY RATATOUILLE

½   cup French dressing
2   cups zucchini slices
½   cup bell pepper strips
2   cups mushrooms slices
1½ cups cherry tomato halves

Pour dressing over combined zucchini and green pepper. Simmer 10 minutes; add mushrooms and tomatoes. Continue cooking just until mushrooms are tender. Yields; 6 - 8 servings.

RICE CASSEROLE

3   cups cooked rice
1   10 ounce jar Alfredo sauce
½   cup milk
2   cups cooked chicken
1   can Leseur peas
⅓   cup roasted red pepper
¼   cup almonds, optional
1   teaspoon basil
1   cup bread crumbs

Mix and place in casserole dish. Bake covered for 30 minutes at 350 degrees. Remove cover, mix 1 cup bread crumbs and put over top, drizzle with butter and bake for 20 minutes uncovered.

SAUCY POTATO – TOMATO CASSEROLE

6   medium potatoes peeled and quartered
1   16 ounce can stewed tomatoes
1   small onion thinly sliced
¼   cup bell pepper chopped
1   4 ounce can green chilies
cheese sauce
½   cup cracker crumbs
1   tablespoon butter

> Cook potatoes in boiling salted water; drain. Drain tomatoes, reserving ⅓ cup juice. Combine tomatoes, reserved juice, potatoes, onion, green pepper, green chilies, and seasonings in a large bowl. Spoon into a greased 2 quart casserole dish. Top with cheese sauce. Sprinkle with cracker crumbs and dot with butter. Cover and bake at 350 degrees for 25 minutes. Remove cover, bake 5 additional minutes.

CHEESE SAUCE

2   tablespoons butter
2   tablespoons flour
½   cup milk
½   cup Cheddar cheese, grated
2   tablespoons mayonnaise
½   teaspoon salt

> Melt butter in small saucepan; blend in flour and cook over low heat, stirring constantly until smooth. Gradually add milk; cook over medium heat, stirring constantly, until thickened. Add cheese, stir until melted. Add remaining ingredients, remove from heat.

SCALLOPED POTATOES

4   cups sliced white potatoes
2   tablespoons butter
1   can cream of mushroom soup
1   can evaporated milk
1   medium onion, sliced in rings
1   medium bell pepper, chopped

Place ½ of potatoes in 1 ½ quart casserole dish, dot with butter. Add onion and bell pepper. Combine soup and milk; pour half of mixture over potatoes. Repeat layers with remaining potatoes, butter and soup mixture. Cover, bake in 325 degree oven for about 1 hour. Remove cover, continue baking 15 minutes or until potatoes are done and lightly browned.

SHOE PEG CORN CASSEROLE

1   stick butter
1   medium onion, chopped
1   small bell pepper, chopped
1   can cream of mushroom soup
2   cans shoe peg corn
2   cups cooked rice
1   jar diced pimentos
2-3 drops Tabasco
¼   teaspoon Worcestershire sauce

Sauté onions and pepper in butter. Mix all ingredients together and top with grated cheese. Bake at 350 degrees until bubbly.

SHREDDED YAMS

2   pounds raw sweet potatoes
1   gallon water
1   tablespoon salt
½   cup white corn syrup
1   cup sugar
½   cup water
1   cup pineapple juice
4   tablespoons butter

Shred yams into gallon of water and salt. Combine sugar, syrup and ½ cup water in saucepan; cook until it forms a light syrup. Drain potatoes, rinse and pat dry. Place in baking dish; pour pineapple juice over it, then cooked syrup. Dot with butter. Bake uncovered for 35 minutes at 350 degrees until potatoes are translucent.

SIMPLE POTATOES

2½ pounds red potatoes
1   stick butter, melted
seasoning salt
garlic salt

Peel and cut potatoes into cubes. Place in microwave safe dish. Pour melted butter over potatoes. Sprinkle with seasoning salt and garlic salt. Bake in microwave until potatoes are tender, stirring occasionally.

SPINACH – BROCCOLI CASSEROLE

2   10 ounce packages frozen chopped spinach
2   10 ounce packages frozen chopped broccoli
2   cups sour cream
1   package dry onion soup mix
salt and pepper to taste
½   cup grated Cheddar cheese

> Cook spinach and broccoli according to package directions; drain well. Combine sour cream and soup mix; stir into spinach and broccoli. Season with salt and pepper. Place in casserole dish. Bake covered, in preheated 325 degrees oven for 40 minutes. Remove from oven. Top with cheese and place back into oven to melt cheese.

SQUASH CASSEROLE

2-3 cups cooked squash
1   egg, beaten
½   cup butter
½   cup mayonnaise
1   tablespoon sugar
2   cups grated Cheddar cheese, divided
1½ cups Ritz cracker crumbs, divided
dash cayenne pepper
salt and pepper to taste

> Mix egg, butter, mayonnaise, sugar and ½ of the cheese and ½ of cracker crumbs. Season with salt, pepper and cayenne. Add squash. Place in buttered casserole dish; top with remaining cheese and cracker crumbs. Bake at 350 degrees for 30 - 35 minutes.

SUPREME SQUASH CASSEROLE

4   cups sliced yellow squash
3   cups fresh ripe tomatoes, crushed
1   large onion, chopped
1   tablespoon oregano
1   stick butter, melted
1   teaspoon coarse ground pepper
½   teaspoon garlic salt
½   teaspoon Tabasco
salt to taste
1   cup sharp Cheddar cheese

Place all ingredients except cheese in large baking dish. Cook, covered, for approximately ½ hour or until squash are tender. Remove cover; stir in cheese, continue cooking uncovered until cheese melts and mixture thickens slightly, approximately ½ hour. Stir to mix melted cheese into casserole.

SWEET POTATO BALLS

2   cups hot mashed sweet potatoes
¼   cup pineapple juice
crushed corn flakes

Measure cooked potatoes, add pineapple juice and beat until smooth. Form into balls the size of small eggs. Roll in corn flake crumbs. Place in a buttered shallow baking dish and bake at 325 degrees for 25 minutes.

TOMATO CHEESE BAKE

8   medium ripe tomatoes, sliced
2   cups grated Cheddar cheese
2   medium onions, thinly sliced
1   teaspoon salt
½   teaspoon pepper
1   cup potato chips, crushed

Arrange half of tomato slices in bottom of casserole dish. Arrange ½ of cheese and onion slices in layers over tomatoes. Sprinkle with ½ salt and pepper. Repeat layers. Top with crushed potato chips. Bake at 350 degrees until onions are tender. Yields; 8 servings.

TOMATO NAPOLEON

3   large tomatoes
salt
dried basil
Mozzarella cheese, shredded
broken salad greens
fresh tomato dressing

Spray jelly-roll pan with cooking spray. Slice tomatoes into ½ inch thickness. Place slices on pan. Sprinkle with salt and basil. Let sit for 5 minutes. Place approximately 2 tablespoons of Mozzarella on each slice of tomato. Stack tomatoes two high. Place in preheated 350 degree oven 10 minutes. Remove when cheese is melted. Place on a small amount of salad greens. Cover with 2 - 3 tablespoons of Fresh Tomato dressing, page 42. Yields; 6 servings. This is great served with chicken croissant sandwiches.

VEGETABLE CASSEROLE

1   10 ounce package frozen broccoli
1   10 ounce package frozen cauliflower
1   10 ounce package frozen sliced carrots
1   can cream of celery soup
½   pound Velveeta cheese, cubed
½   package Pepperidge Farm stuffing
1   stick butter, melted

Cook vegetables according to directions. Drain, place in 2 quart baking dish. Add cubed cheese and undiluted soup. Stir lightly to mix. Cover with stuffing mix. Pour melted butter over stuffing mix. Bake 30 minutes at 350 degrees.

VIDALIA ONION PIE

20   saltine crackers, crushed
3   tablespoons butter, melted
2   cups sliced onion
2   eggs
2   tablespoons milk
grated cheese

Sauté onions in butter until tender. Mix saltines and melted butter and pat into pie plate to form crust. Place sautéed onions over crust. Beat the eggs and milk together and pour over onions. Top with grated cheese. Bake at 350 degrees until cheese melts.

WILD RICE CASSEROLE

1 cup wild rice
1 10 ounce can beef broth
1 10 ounce can onion soup
1 stick butter, melted
1 6 ounce can mushrooms, chopped

Mix all ingredients and pour into casserole dish. Cover and bake at 350 degrees for 30 minutes. Stir with folk and continue cooking for 30 more minutes. This is also good with 1 cup white rice instead of wild rice.

MAIN
DISHES

Index

SPINACH LASAGNA

½   package uncooked lasagna
2   tablespoons olive oil
¾   cup chopped onion
2   cloves garlic, finely chopped
2   29 ounce jars prepared spaghetti sauce
1   16 ounce carton Ricotta cheese
1   10 ounce package frozen spinach, thawed and well drained
1   pound shredded Mozzarella cheese, divided
½   cup grated Parmesan cheese
2   eggs, beaten
chopped parsley

> Prepare lasagna according to package directions, drain. In large saucepan, heat oil. Add onions and garlic, cook until tender. Stir in spaghetti sauce, simmer uncovered 15 minutes. In medium bowl, combine Ricotta, spinach, ½ cup Mozzarella, Parmesan, and eggs, mix well. In a 15 x 9 inch baking dish, layer 2 cups sauce, half the lasagna, half the remaining sauce, all of the spinach mixture, half of the remaining Mozzarella, remaining lasagna, and sauce. Cover, bake at 350 degrees until bubbly, about 45 minutes. Uncover, top with remaining Mozzarella and parsley. Bake 15 minutes. Let stand 10 minutes before serving.

TURKEY BREAST

1   Butterball turkey breast with ribs
garlic salt
salt

Place turkey breast in crock pot. Cover with garlic salt and a little salt. Add 1 cup water. Cook in crock pot until falling apart. Place in dish and pour broth over turkey.

BEEF

BAKED ZITI

1   tablespoon butter
2   cloves garlic, minced
1   pound lean ground beef
1   24 ounce jar tomato and basil pasta sauce
¾   teaspoon salt, divided
1   16 ounce box Ziti pasta
3   tablespoons butter
3   tablespoons all purpose flour
3   cups milk
1   cup grated Parmesan cheese
1   teaspoon pepper
1   8 ounce package shredded Mozzarella

In large skillet, place 1 tablespoon butter and ground beef. Brown beef until no longer pink. Drain beef mixture and return to pan. Stir in pasta sauce and ½ teaspoon salt. Set aside. Cook pasta in a large Dutch oven according to package directions. Drain and return to Dutch oven. Melt butter in heavy saucepan over low heat, whisk in flour until smooth. Cook, whisking constantly, 1 minute. Gradually whisk in milk. Cook over medium heat, whisking constantly, until mixture is thick and bubbly. Stir in Parmesan cheese, remaining ¼ teaspoon salt and pepper. Pour sauce over pasta in Dutch oven stirring until pasta is evenly coated. Transfer pasta mixture to a lightly greased 13 x 9 inch baking dish. Top evenly with beef mixture, sprinkle evenly with Mozzarella cheese. Bake at 350 degrees for 20 - 25 minutes or until cheese is melted. Let stand 10 minutes before serving.

BARBECUED MEAT LOAF

1½ pounds ground beef
1   cup dry bread crumbs
1   large onion, chopped
1   egg, beaten
1½ teaspoons salt
¼   teaspoon pepper
2   8 ounce cans tomato sauce
½   cup water
3   tablespoons vinegar
2   tablespoons prepared mustard
3   tablespoons brown sugar
2   teaspoons Worcestershire sauce

Mix ground beef, crumbs, onion, egg, salt, pepper and 1 can of tomato sauce together. Form into a loaf and place in loaf pan or baking dish. Combine remaining ingredients mix well. Pour over loaf. Bake at 350 degrees for 1 hour and 30 minutes, basting several times during baking.

BEEF ROAST IN MUSHROOM GRAVY

5   pounds Sirloin tip roast
2   10 ¾ ounce cans cream of mushroom soup
2   envelopes Lipton Onion Soup Mix
¾   cup water

Place roast in crock pot. Blend mushroom soup, onion soup mix and water together; pour over roast. Cover and cook on high for 7 - 8 hours or until roast is tender. In oven cook at 250 degrees until tender. Serve gravy with rice or potatoes.

CHEESY BEEF ENCHILADAS

1   pound ground beef
1   16 ounce jar thick and chunky salsa, divided
1   8 ounce package Cheddar and Monterey Jack cheese
Mexican style shredded cheese, divided
10 flour tortillas

Brown meat; drain. Stir in ½ cup salsa and 1 cup cheese. Spread
1 cup salsa in a 9 x 13 inch baking dish. Place ¼ cup meat
mixture down the center of each tortilla; roll up. Place tortillas,
seam side down, on salsa. Top with remaining ½ cup salsa and
1 cup cheese. Bake at 350 degrees for 20 - 25 minutes or until
thoroughly heated.

CHILI

2   pounds ground beef
2   medium onions, chopped
2   cans kidney beans
2   8 ounce cans tomato sauce
2   16 ounce cans tomatoes
4   tablespoons chili powder
1   bay leaf
salt, pepper and garlic salt

Brown meat in small amount of oil. Add other ingredients.
Bring to a boil then reduce to simmer and cook approximately
2 hours.

COMPANY CASSEROLE

1   pound ground beef, browned
1   medium onion, sliced
6   medium potatoes, sliced
1   can cream of mushroom soup
½   cup evaporated milk
salt and pepper to taste

Arrange hamburger, onion and potatoes in layers in casserole. Season to taste. Mix soup and milk together and pour over top. Cover, bake at 375 degrees for 45 minutes to 1 hour until potatoes are tender. Yields; 4 serving.

EGGPLANT CASSEROLE

2   cups ground beef
1   tablespoon butter
2   cups cooked eggplant, mashed
2   cups cooked rice
1   10 ounce can cream of mushroom soup
salt and pepper to taste
½   cup crushed saltine crackers

Sauté ground beef in butter until it changes color. Add other ingredients except cracker crumbs. Put in buttered casserole dish and top with cracker crumbs. Bake at 350 degrees for 25 - 30 minutes. Serve hot.

EGGPLANT PARMIGIANA

2	tablespoons salad oil	1	tablespoons brown sugar
½	cup chopped onion	1	large eggplant
1	clove garlic, crushed	2	eggs, slightly beaten
½	pound ground beef	½	cup Italian flavored bread
2	16 ounce cans Italian		crumbs
	tomatoes, un-drained	1¼	cups grated Parmesan
1	6 ounce can tomato paste		cheese
2	teaspoons oregano	⅓	cup salad oil
1	teaspoon basil leaves	1	8 ounce package
1½	teaspoons salt		Mozzarella cheese slices
¼	teaspoon pepper		

In two tablespoons hot oil in large skillet, sauté onion, garlic and ground beef until meat is no longer red. Add tomatoes, tomato paste, oregano, basil, salt, pepper and sugar. Bring to boiling stirring with wooden spoon; reduce heat, simmer, stirring occasionally for 45 minutes. Preheat oven to 350 degrees. Lightly grease a 13 x 9 x 2 inch baking dish. Wash eggplant. Do not peel. Cut into sections ¼ inch thick. In pie plate, combine eggs and 1 tablespoon water, mix well with fork. On wax paper, combine bread crumbs and ½ cup Parmesan cheese; mix well. Dip eggplant slices in egg mixture, coating well. Then dip in crumb mixture. In 1 tablespoon hot oil in skillet, sauté eggplant slices until golden brown and crisp on both sides. Add more oil as needed. Arrange half of eggplant slices on bottom of prepared baking dish. Sprinkle with half of the remaining Parmesan cheese. Top with half of Mozzarella cheese slices. Cover with half of tomato sauce. Arrange remaining eggplant slices over tomato sauce, cover with rest of tomato sauce and Mozzarella cheese. Sprinkle top with rest of Parmesan cheese. Bake uncovered 25 minutes or until cheese melts and top is browned. You may make ahead, bake and freeze.

HAMBURGER PIE

1 pound ground beef
1 medium onion, chopped
1 teaspoon salt
2 teaspoons chili powder
dash Worcestershire sauce
1 15 ounce can tomatoes
1 15 ounce can English peas
1 15 ounce can whole potatoes, diced
1 15 ounce can whole kernel corn
1 cup cornmeal
1 tablespoon salt
1 tablespoon baking powder
1 egg, beaten
1½ cups buttermilk

Brown beef in skillet, along with onion, salt, chili powder and Worcestershire sauce. Drain liquid from vegetables. Spread meat mixture in bottom of an oiled 3 quart baking dish; combine drained vegetables and spread over meat. Combine cornmeal, flour, salt and baking powder. Stir in beaten egg and buttermilk. Mix well and spoon over vegetable layer. Bake at 400 degrees for 30 - 45 minutes or until brown. Yields; 8 - 10 serving.

HAMBURGER POTATO CASSEROLE

1	pound ground beef
3	cups peeled and thinly sliced potatoes
1	can cream of mushroom soup
½	cup chopped onion
¾	cup milk

salt to taste

freshly ground pepper to taste

1	cup shredded Cheddar cheese

Preheat oven to 350 degrees. In a medium skillet over medium heat, brown the ground beef; then drain. In a medium mixing bowl, combine cream of mushroom soup, onion, milk, salt and pepper. Alternately layer the potatoes, soup mixture and meat in an 11 x 7 inch baking dish. Bake in the oven for 1 - 1 ½ hours or until potatoes are tender. Top with Cheddar cheese, and continue baking until cheese is melted.

IRISH STEW

small amount of oil
1½ pounds lean boneless stew beef
2 cups water
1 medium onion
½ cup celery, chopped
4 carrots, chopped
3 potatoes, peeled and cut into small pieces
1 29 ounce can diced tomatoes
1 8 ounce can tomato sauce
1 14 ounce can cut green beans and juice
1 tablespoon sugar
salt and pepper to taste

Flour stew beef and brown in oil in Dutch oven. Add water and cook on low heat for 1 hour. Add other ingredients and bring to boil. Cut heat to low and cook for approximately 2 hours or until meat is tender. This may also be cooked in a crock pot until meat is tender.

ITALIAN SPAGHETTI SAUCE

2   pounds ground beef
4   6 ounce cans tomato paste
2   8 ounce cans tomato sauce
¼   cup Worcestershire sauce
½   cup ketchup
1   tablespoon oregano
2   large onions, diced
salt, pepper and garlic salt
2   large bell peppers, chopped
1   cup sliced mushrooms
1   bunch celery, chopped
juice of 1 lemon

Brown meat in ¼ stick of butter. Add other ingredients, bring to a boil. Turn to simmer and cook for 2 hours. Serve over spaghetti.

ITALIAN STYLE MEATLOAF

shortening for preparing baking dish

2   pounds ground beef

1   large onion, finely chopped

2   packages beefy onion soup mix

3   eggs, beaten

1   cup Italian bread crumbs

2   cups marinara sauce, divided

½   teaspoon garlic powder

½   teaspoon black pepper

½   teaspoon salt

½   teaspoon oregano

Preheat oven to 375 degrees. Grease a loaf pan and set aside. Mix ground beef, onion, soup mix, eggs, Italian bread crumbs, 1 cup marinara sauce, garlic powder, black pepper, salt, and oregano. Form into a loaf. Place loaf in center of greased pan. Cover with foil and bake for 1 hour or until center of loaf is firm. Remove cover, pour remaining marinara sauce on top and bake uncovered for 15 minutes. Remove from oven and let set 10 minutes before serving. Yields; 4 - 6 servings.

LASAGNE

MEAT SAUCE

1   tablespoon corn oil
½   pound ground beef
¾   cup chopped onion
2   cloves minced garlic
5   cups prepared meatless spaghetti sauce
¼   cup chopped parsley

In a 3 quart saucepan, heat corn oil. Add ground beef, onion, and garlic; sauté 10 minutes or until meat is no longer pink. Add spaghetti sauce and parsley; bring to a boil. Reduce heat, simmer 15 minutes.

FILLING

2   15 ounce cartons Ricotta cheese
2   eggs, slightly beaten
1   cup grated Parmesan cheese, divided
2   cups shredded Mozzarella cheese, divided
1   16 ounce package lasagna noodles cooked drained

In medium bowl, combine Ricotta, eggs, ¾ cup Parmesan and 1 ½ cups Mozzarella. Spread 1 cup meat sauce into a 13 x 9 inch baking dish. Layer ¼ of the lasagna noodles, ⅓ of the Ricotta mixture and 1 cup meat sauce. Repeat twice. Top with remaining lasagna noodles, meat sauce, ½ cup Mozzarella and ¼ cup Parmesan. Cover. Bake in 375 degree oven for 35 minutes, uncover and bake 15 minutes longer. Let stand 15 minutes before serving. Yields; 12 servings.

LIVER GERMAN STYLE

6	slices bacon	1	pound liver in ½ inch slices
2	tablespoons finely chopped onion	¼	cup flour
		1	teaspoon salt
3	tablespoons vinegar	1	teaspoon sugar

Cook bacon until crisp. Remove from frying pan and break into pieces. Dredge liver in seasoned flour. Brown slowly on both sides in bacon drippings until done. Remove liver to hot platter. Add onions, vinegar and sugar to drippings. Bring to a boil; cook one minute and pour over liver. Top with bacon.

PEPPER STEAK

1	cup onion	1	cup bell pepper
1	cup celery	1	small can water chestnuts
1	cup beef consommé	1	stick butter
1	tablespoon paprika		garlic salt
2	large fresh tomatoes		tenderizer
¼	cup soy sauce	¼	cup water
2-3	tablespoons cornstarch	1	pound round steak

Slice steak in thin strips and sprinkle with paprika, garlic and tenderizer. Brown sliced steak in butter, add vegetables and stir fry until crisp, add soup and bring to a boil. Mix soy sauce, water, cornstarch, and pour in to thicken. Cut fresh tomatoes in 8ths or 10ths. Add last and turn off. OPTIONAL VEGETABLES; Add to your taste. broccoli, cauliflower, mushrooms, and squash.

RANGER CASSEROLE

1	pound ground round steak
1	cup sliced onions
½	cup bell peppers, diced
1	15 ounce can tomatoes
1	8 ounce can tomato sauce
½	cup uncooked rice
1	teaspoon chili powder
1½	teaspoons salt
¼	teaspoon pepper
½	cup diced celery

Brown meat; add other ingredients and bring to a boil. Turn into greased casserole dish. Cover and bake at 350 degrees for 1 hour or until rice is tender. Add more liquid if necessary.

SPANISH SPAGHETTI

1½	pounds ground round steak
1	large onion, chopped
1	large bell pepper, chopped
1	8 ounce box spaghetti
1	29 ounce can tomatoes
1	10 ounce can cream of celery soup
1	10 ounce can cream of mushroom soup
1	21 ounce bottle ketchup

Brown meat in 2 tablespoons oil; season with salt, pepper, garlic salt, bell pepper and chopped onion. Flatten this mixture out in pot. Break spaghetti and lay on top of meat. Put tomatoes and soup over spaghetti. Pour ketchup over all. Cover tight; bring to a boil, cut to low heat and simmer for 1 hour. Do not remove lid and do not stir.

STUFFED PEPPERS ITALIAN STYLE

6   large bell peppers
2   cups cooked rice
2   cups ground beef, cooked
1   small onion, chopped fine
salt and pepper to taste
1   cup ketchup
1   8 ounce can tomato sauce
½   cup Italian bread crumbs
1   16 ounce jar Ragu Italian Cooking Sauce

Cut off the stem ends of peppers; remove seeds. Boil peppers for 5 minutes in lightly salted water; drain. Mix together all other ingredients except the jar of Ragu Italian Cooking Sauce. Stuff mixture into the peppers. Spoon the jar of Italian Cooking Sauce over tops of peppers. Bake at 325 degrees for 30 minutes.

TACO CASSEROLE

1   2 ounce envelope chili seasoning mix
1   pound ground beef
1   16 ounce can tomatoes
1   16 ounce can kidney beans
1½ cups broken Fritos
1   cup Cheddar cheese, grated
2   cups shredded lettuce

Prepare chili according to package directions using ground beef, tomatoes and kidney beans. Spoon into shallow 2 quart casserole dish. Sprinkle with cheese. Top with broken Fritos. Bake at 350 degrees for 15 minutes or until cheese melts and casserole is bubbling hot. Serve on bed of shredded lettuce.

TACOS

2	dozen prepared taco shells		Ground Beef Filling, below
1	head lettuce, shredded	1	8 ounce package Cheddar
2	medium tomatoes, chopped		cheese, grated
1	bunch green onions, chopped		

Prepare filling. Stuff taco shell with 2 tablespoons of filling. Add tomatoes, lettuce, green onions and sprinkle with cheese and taco sauce.

TACO SAUCE

1	15 ounce can tomatoes	1	2 ounce can green chilies
2	clove garlic	1	small onion, chopped
1	teaspoon salt	¼	teaspoon oregano

Place all ingredients in blender and chop only until mixture is blended.

GROUND BEEF FILLING

1	large onion, chopped	2	pounds ground beef
2	medium tomatoes, chopped	2	teaspoons salt
1	teaspoon pepper	1	tablespoon oregano
2	cloves garlic, crushed		

Brown beef and onion together and be sure to drain off fat. Add remaining ingredients and heat thoroughly hot. I usually simmer for about 30 minutes.

TALLERENE

2   pounds ground beef
½   pound Cheddar cheese
1   pound New York State cheese
1   8 ounce package fine noodles
2   tablespoons shortening
2   medium onions
1   can mexicorn
2   10 ounce cans tomato soup
ketchup

> Melt shortening in skillet; add seasoned hamburger. Add grated onion and sear until no red shows. Add undiluted soup and mexicorn. Boil noodles in salt water for 7 minutes and drain. Mix meat mixture and noodles and stir well. Pour into large baking dish lined on sides and bottom with grated Cheddar cheese. Cut finger sized sticks of New York State cheese and push into casserole dish. Dot top with ketchup. Bake at 350 degrees for 45 minutes. This freezes well.

TATER TOT CASSEROLE

1½   pounds ground beef
1   medium onion
salt to taste
2   14 ounce cans French style green beans, drained
1   10 ounce can cream of mushroom soup
1   12 ounce can evaporated milk
1   bag frozen tater tots

> Brown beef and chopped onion with salt added. Place beef in bottom of a 9 x 13 inch casserole dish. Spread beans over beef. Cover beans with frozen tater tots. Mix together the milk and soup. Spoon over top of casserole. Bake for 1 hour at 325 degrees.

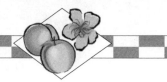

WESETTI CASSEROLE

1½ pounds ground beef
1 small onion finely chopped
salt and pepper to taste
dash Worcestershire Sauce
dash hot sauce
1 5 ounce package fine noodles
½ pound Cheddar cheese, grated
1 10 ¾ ounce can tomato soup
1 10 ¾ ounce can cream of mushroom soup
cracker crumbs
butter

Slightly brown meat and onion. Add salt, pepper and sauces.
Cook slowly until meat is tender. Cook noodles according to
package directions, drain. Add cheese and stir until cheese is
melted. Stir in meat mixture and soup. Pour into greased a
9 x 13 inch casserole. Cover with cracker crumbs, dot with butter. Bake at 350 degrees for 45 minutes.

CHICKEN

CHICKEN – BROCCOLI CASSEROLE

2   10 ounce packages frozen chopped broccoli

8   chicken breasts, cooked and chopped

1   10 ¾ ounce can cream of chicken or cream of mushroom soup

⅔   cup mayonnaise

1   cup Cheddar cheese, grated

1   tablespoon lemon juice

1   teaspoon curry powder

1   cup buttered bread crumbs

Cook broccoli according to package directions; drain well. Place in a lightly greased 1 ½ quart casserole dish, top with chicken. Combine remaining ingredients except bread crumbs, stirring well. Spoon mixture over chicken and top with bread crumbs. Bake at 350 degrees for 30 minutes or until bubbly.

CHICKEN – DRESSING CASSEROLE

8   chicken breast halves
1   can cream of celery soup
1   can cream of mushroom soup
2   cups chicken broth
1   package Pepperidge Farm cornbread stuffing
½   teaspoon salt
¼   teaspoon pepper
1   teaspoon celery salt

Boil chicken until tender and chop. Place chicken in a 9 x 13 inch casserole dish. Dot with butter then sprinkle with salt, pepper and celery salt. Mix soup and broth together and pour over chicken. Cover with stuffing mix. Bake at 350 degrees until bubbly, approximately 30 minutes.

CHICKEN AND VEGETABLE CASSEROLE

2-3 pounds cooked chicken, chopped

2   cans cream of mushroom soup

1   can cream of chicken soup

½   can chicken broth

2   cans veg-all, drained

1   can green beans, drained

1   can corn, drained

⅓   cup mayonnaise

Combine all ingredients together in a 9 x 13 inch baking dish.

TOPPING

2   sleeves Ritz crackers

1½   sticks butter

Top casserole with crumbled Ritz crackers. Cover the entire top of casserole with butter cut into small pats. Bake uncovered at 375 degrees until lightly brown, about 35 minutes.

CHICKEN CASSEROLE

2   cans cream of mushroom soup
refill can with milk
juice of 2 lemons
8   bay leaves
6 - 8chicken breasts, floured and browned on both sides

>Put soup mixture in a 9 x 13 inch dish. Place chicken in mixture and mash down. Drizzle ½ cup melted butter over top. Bake at 250 degrees for 3 hours.

CHICKEN DELICIOUS

8   chicken breasts
2   cans cream of chicken soup
2   8 ounce cartons sour cream
½   can chicken broth
2   sleeves Ritz crackers, crushed
1   stick butter

>Boil chicken breasts until tender. Chop. Mix the chicken soup and sour cream together. Mix into chicken. Add broth. Crumble one sleeve of Ritz crackers in bottom of baking dish. Pour chicken mixture over this and crumble other sleeve of Ritz crackers over top. Melt butter and pour over. Bake at 350 degrees for 30 minutes.

CHICKEN ENCHILADAS

2	cups chicken, cooked and chopped
2	cups sour cream
1	can cream of chicken soup
2	cups Monterey Jack cheese, shredded
2	cups Cheddar cheese, shredded
1	4 ounce can chopped green Chiles, drained
2	tablespoons onion
⅛	teaspoon salt
¼	teaspoon pepper
10	10-inch flour tortillas
1	cup Cheddar cheese, shredded

Combine 1st 9 ingredients. Mix well. Soften tortillas in microwave for about 10 seconds. Place ½ cup chicken mixture on each tortilla and roll up. Place seam side down in a 9 x 13 inch baking dish, recipe will fill 2 dishes. Cover and bake at 350 degrees for 20 minutes. Remove from oven, sprinkle with 1 cup of Cheddar cheese, bake uncovered for an additional 5 minutes.

CHICKEN EUGENE

4   chicken breasts

salt and paprika

8   thin slices cooked ham

½   cup butter, melted

1   10 ¾ ounce can cream of mushroom soup

½   cup sherry

1   8 ounce carton sour cream

1   4 ounce can sliced mushrooms, drained

> Sprinkle chicken with salt and paprika. Place ham slices in a shallow baking dish, top with chicken. Combine remaining ingredients, blending well. Pour over chicken. Bake at 350 degrees for 1 - 1 ½ hours or until done.

CHICKEN TETRAZZINI

1   8 ounce package thin spaghetti
10-12 chicken breast halves, cooked and diced or
5   cups diced chicken
2   10 ounce cans cream of mushroom soup, undiluted
2   teaspoons Worcestershire sauce
¼   teaspoon nutmeg
1   cup mayonnaise
½   cup sherry
½   cup whipping cream, whipped
½-1 cup slivered almonds
2   teaspoons butter
½   cup grated Parmesan cheese

Preheat oven to 350 degrees. Cook spaghetti according to package directions. Drain and place in a shallow casserole dish. Spread chicken over spaghetti. Toast almonds in butter and sprinkle over chicken. Make a sauce with all remaining ingredients except cheese. Pour sauce over contents of casserole and top with Parmesan cheese. Bake for 30 minutes. Yields 12 servings. This can be made a day ahead or it can be frozen. It is a good dish to take to a friend.

CHICKEN IMPERIAL

6   chicken breasts
1   teaspoon salt
¾   cup butter, melted
2   teaspoons Worcestershire sauce
1-2   teaspoons curry powder
1   teaspoon oregano
½   teaspoon dry mustard
½   teaspoon garlic powder
¼   teaspoon paprika
2-3   drops hot sauce
⅓   cup sherry

Sprinkle chicken with salt and place skin side down in a greased 13 x 9 x 2 inch baking dish. Combine rest of ingredients, mixing well; brush over chicken. Bake at 350 degrees for 1 hour or until tender. Turn and baste with pan drippings several times.

CHICKEN LASAGNA

1   8 ounce package medium egg noodles, uncooked
½   cup butter
½   cup all purpose flour
1   teaspoon salt
½   teaspoon pepper
1   teaspoon dried basil
4   cups chicken broth
4   cups chopped cooked chicken breasts
1   24 ounce carton cottage cheese
1   large egg
2   8 ounce packages shredded Mozzarella cheese
¾   cup grated Parmesan cheese

Cook noodles according to package directions; drain and set aside. Melt butter in a large saucepan over medium heat; stir in flour and next 3 ingredients. Cook, stirring constantly, 1 - 2 minutes. Add broth, stirring until smooth, bring to a boil. Reduce heat and simmer 5 - 8 minutes or until thick and bubbly. Stir in chicken, remove from heat. Combine cottage cheese and egg, stirring well. Spoon one third of chicken mixture in bottom of lightly greased 9 x 13 inch dish. Top with half of noodles, half of cottage cheese mixture and 1 cup Mozzarella cheese. Repeat layers, ending with chicken mixture. Sprinkle Parmesan cheese on top. Bake at 350 degrees for 1 hour. Yields; 8 servings.

CHICKEN N DUMPLINGS

2   packages boneless chicken breasts, cooked and shredded
1   12 ounce package Mary B's Open Kettle dumplings
6-8 medium potatoes
1   tablespoon tarragon leaves
salt to taste

> Boil chicken breast in salted water until tender. Take out of broth and set aside. Shred the chicken. Bring 3 ½ - 4 quarts of the broth to a rolling boil. Drop dumplings in and reduce heat to medium and cook for 40 - 45 minutes until tender. Add tarragon leaves. Cook potatoes in separate saucepan in salted water until tender. When dumplings are tender, add shredded chicken and potatoes. Let stand 15 minutes before serving.

CHICKEN PARMESAN

4   chicken breasts, skinned and boned
1   large egg, slightly beaten
½   cup Italian seasoned bread crumbs
2   tablespoons butter
1¾   cups 6 Cheese's prepared spaghetti sauce
½   cup shredded Mozzarella cheese
1   tablespoon grated Parmesan cheese

> Place chicken between 2 sheets of heavy duty plastic wrap. Flatten to ¼ inch thickness, using a meat mallet or rolling pin. Dip in egg, dredge in crumbs. Melt butter in a skillet over medium high heat; add chicken. Cook 2 minutes on each side or until browned. Pour spaghetti sauce over chicken. Cover, reduce heat and simmer 20 minutes. Top with cheeses. Cover; simmer 5 minutes or until Mozzarella cheese melts. Yields; 4 servings.

CHICKEN PIE

6   chicken breasts, cooked and cut up
1¾   cups broth
1   10 ¾ ounce can cream of celery soup
1   stick butter, melted
1   cup self rising flour
¾   cup milk
salt and pepper to taste

Place chicken in a 9 x 13 inch baking dish. Pour broth over chicken. Spread soup over chicken and broth. Sprinkle with salt and pepper. Mix melted butter, flour and milk together; pour over soup and spread evenly. Bake at 350 degrees for 40 minutes, or until brown crust forms.

CHICKEN ROLL UPS

2   8 ounce packages crescent rolls
3   chicken breasts
1   can cream of chicken soup
2   cups shredded cheese

Cook chicken until tender and shred. Mix together chicken, soup and 2 cups cheese. Place in crescent rolls and bake according to directions.

CHICKEN ROYAL

8   boneless chicken breasts
1   12 ounce package cream cheese, softened
1   stick butter, melted
3   tablespoons frozen chives
salt and pepper

> Pound chicken breasts. Place 2-3 tablespoons cream cheese in the middle of chicken. Sprinkle with frozen chives, salt and pepper. Roll chicken up. Place in baking dish. Pour melted butter over chicken. Cover and cook at 425 degrees for 45 minutes. Remove cover and continue cooking for 15 minutes more.

CHICKEN SALAD CASSEROLE

6   chicken breasts, cooked and cut up
1   cup chopped celery
1   cup cooked rice
1   10 ounce can cream of chicken soup
2   teaspoons dried onions
½   cup slivered almonds
1   cup sliced water chestnuts
½   cup mayonnaise
1   teaspoon salt

> Mix together and pour into casserole dish. Cover top with crushed potato chips. Bake at 450 degrees for 30-35 minutes.

CHICKEN SPAGHETTI CASSEROLE

1 8 ounce package spaghetti
2 bell peppers, chopped
1 large onion, chopped
1 pound mushrooms, sliced
1 tablespoon olive oil
1 29 ounce can tomatoes, un-drained
1 cup sour cream
2 cups cooked chicken, chopped
salt and pepper to taste
1 cup grated sharp Cheddar cheese

Preheat oven to 350 degrees. Cook spaghetti according to package directions. Drain and put in a large 3 quart buttered casserole dish. While spaghetti is cooking, sauté peppers, onion and mushrooms in oil until onion is clear. Combine tomatoes and sour cream and pour over spaghetti, mixing well. Add chicken and sautéed vegetables. Add salt and pepper, mixing all ingredients well. Top with cheese and bake 30 - 45 minutes or until bubbly. Yields; 8 - 10 servings.

CHICKEN STROGONOFF

6	chicken breasts	salt, pepper and paprika to taste
1/3	cup vegetable oil	2	medium onions, chopped
1/2	cup chicken bouillon	1	tablespoon prepared mustard
1	16 ounce can tomato sauce	1	can chopped mushrooms
1	8 ounce carton sour cream		

Season chicken with salt, pepper and paprika. Brown both sides in oil. Set aside. Brown onions slightly. Add bouillon, mustard, tomato sauce and mushrooms. Cover and simmer 45 minutes. Move chicken to platter. Add sour cream to sauce and heat. Do not boil. Pour over chicken and serve with rice.

CHICKEN-A-LA-KING

6	chicken breasts cooked and chopped	1⅓ cups chicken broth
1/2	cup bell peppers, chopped	1	cup mushrooms
1/4	cup pimentos, chopped	4	tablespoons self rising flour
1	cup milk	1/4	almond slivers, optional
salt and pepper to taste	2	egg yolks
	2	teaspoons sherry, optional

Heat ⅓ cup broth. Add mushrooms and peppers and cook about 5 minutes on low heat or until soft. Add flour and stir well. Add 1 cup broth and milk gradually. Beat egg yolks, then add a little of the hot mixture to the yolks to heat them, then add back to mixture. Add chopped pimentos, salt, pepper, sherry, and almond slivers. Add chopped chicken to sauce and spoon into individual tart shells, pie crust or serve over toast.

COUNTRY CAPTAIN

6   chicken breasts
flour, salt and pepper
shortening
1   medium onion, chopped
1   medium bell pepper, chopped
1   small garlic bud, minced
¾   teaspoon salt
¼   teaspoon white pepper
1½ tablespoons currants
1½ teaspoons curry powder
1   29 ounce can tomatoes
1   teaspoon chopped parsley
¼   teaspoon thyme
½   cup almonds, toasted

Remove skin from chicken, roll in mixture of flour, salt and pepper. Brown in melted shortening. Remove chicken from pan, but keep it warm, this is important. Pour all but about 2 tablespoons shortening from pan. Put onions, pepper, and garlic in pan; cook very slowly, stirring constantly. Season with the curry, salt and pepper. Add tomatoes, parsley and thyme. Put chicken in a roaster pan and pour mixture over it. If it does not cover the chicken, rinse out the skillet with water and add to chicken. Bake, uncovered at 350 degrees for about 45 minutes or until chicken is tender. Before serving, drop the currants and almonds in sauce. Serve the sauce over rice.

CRANBERRY CHICKEN SUPREME

6   chicken breast halves
1   can jellied cranberry sauce
2   tablespoons soy sauce
1½   teaspoons lemon juice
½   stick butter

Mix together cranberry sauce, soy sauce, lemon juice, and butter. Melt and mix until smooth. Pour over chicken breast. Bake uncovered at 425 degrees for 30 minutes, turn chicken and bake for 20 minutes.

CREAMY CHICKEN ENCHILADAS

1   tablespoon butter
1   4 ounce can chopped green Chiles, drained
1   8 ounce package cream cheese, softened
3½   cups chopped cooked chicken breasts
8   8 inch flour tortillas
2   8 ounce packages Monterey Jack cheese, shredded
2   cups whipping cream

Melt butter in a large skillet over medium heat. Add Chiles and sauté 1 minute. Stir in cream cheese and chicken; cook, stirring constantly until cheese melts. Spoon 2 - 3 tablespoons chicken mixture down center of each tortilla. Roll up tortillas, place seam side down, in a lightly greased 13 x 9 inch baking dish. Sprinkle with Monterey Jack cheese; drizzle with whipping cream. Bake at 350 degrees for 45 minutes.

DURKEES CHICKEN

8   chicken breasts halves
1   bottle Durkee Sandwich & Salad Sauce
¾   stick butter, melted
juice of 3 lemons

Place chicken breast in crock pot. Heat Durkees, butter and lemon juice. Pour over chicken. Cook on high 5 - 6 hours. This may also be prepared in the oven. Cover and bake at 300 degrees for 1 ½ hours or until tender. Remove cover last 15 minutes of baking time. Serve sauce over rice. Yellow rice is my favorite. If time permits, let chicken stand for 1 hour or so in the sauce before baking, it's even better.

EASY CHICKEN BAKE

2   chicken breast halves
2   small slices butter
2   tablespoons lemon juice
3   tablespoons soy sauce
1   tablespoon Worcestershire sauce

Place chicken breast, meaty side down on a sheet of tin foil. Place pat of margarine on each and pour the soy sauce mixture over. Wrap tightly, place in baking dish and bake at 350 degrees for approximately 1 hour or until tender. If using more chicken, wrap in two's. This freezes well in the same foil it was baked in.

EASY CHICKEN CASSEROLE

1   can cream of mushroom soup
1   can cream of celery soup
1   can cream of chicken soup
6   chicken breasts
butter
½   cup uncooked rice

Mix soup together and spoon into oblong casserole. Mix rice and soup mixture. Place chicken on top of soup mixture and rub butter on top of chicken. Cover and bake 1 hour at 400 degrees.

FLAVORFUL FRIED CHICKEN

chicken breast
garlic salt
seasoning salt
mesquite chicken seasoning
Dales Seasoning Sauce

Season chicken breast with garlic salt, salt, seasoning salt, and mesquite chicken seasoning. Allow to sit. When about ready to fry, marinate with Dales Seasoning Sauce. Dip in buttermilk, then flour, and deep fry until brown.

HOT CHICKEN
ALMOND CROISSANT

7	large chicken breasts	5	tablespoons olive oil
1	medium onion, thinly sliced	1	cup sliced mushrooms
1	teaspoon salt	½	teaspoon pepper
1	teaspoon garlic powder	1	can cream of chicken soup
½	cup water	1	cup sliced almonds
2	cups Mozzarella cheese, shredded	12	large deli croissants
		12	tablespoons mayonnaise

Cut chicken breast into ½ inch strips. Sprinkle with ½ teaspoon salt, garlic powder, and ¼ teaspoon pepper. Toss to ensure strips have been seasoned. Heat 3 tablespoons olive oil in skillet on medium temperature. Place chicken in skillet and cook for approximately 10 minutes or until juices are clear and chicken is no longer pink and just beginning to brown. Turn chicken 2 - 3 times to lightly brown on all sides. Cover and reduce heat to a low simmer. In Dutch oven, heat 2 tablespoons olive oil at medium temperature. Add onion and mushroom slices. Sprinkle with ½ teaspoon salt, garlic powder, and pepper. Sauté onion and mushrooms 3 - 4 minutes. Transfer chicken strips to Dutch oven. Stir in cream of chicken soup and water. Cover and simmer until liquid is reduced to semi-thick gravy consistency. Add to chicken mixture 1 cup cheese and ½ cup almonds. Cover to melt cheese while you prepare croissants. Slice open croissants lengthwise, leaving spine of croissant intact. Spread inside of each croissant with 1 tablespoon of mayonnaise. With slotted spoon, put a generous portion of chicken mixture on each roll. Sprinkle inside of each chicken croissant with remaining cheese and almonds. Place croissant on lightly greased jelly roll pan or cookie sheet in 350 degree oven for 10 - 15 minutes or until cheese is melted and sandwich is thoroughly heated. Place sandwich on plate. Serve immediately. If you have leftover chicken mixture, it can be refrigerated up to 3 days. Yields; 10 - 12 servings.

HOT CHICKEN SALAD SPECIALTY

2   cups cooked chicken, cubed

2   cups celery, chopped

½   cup toasted almonds, chopped

½   teaspoon salt

2   tablespoons onion, grated

½   cup bell pepper, chopped

½   cup mayonnaise

3   tablespoons pimento, chopped

2   tablespoons lemon juice

½   cup cream of chicken soup

½   cup Cheddar cheese, grated

3   cups crushed potato chips

Combine all ingredients except cheese and potato chips. Toss lightly and place in 1 ½ quart greased casserole dish. Spread cheese and potato chips on top. Bake uncovered until heated thoroughly and browned on top.

MEXICAN CHICKEN

6-8 chicken breasts cooked until tender and chopped

1   bag nacho flavored Doritos

1   can Rotel

1   can cream of mushroom soup

1   can cream of chicken soup

1   cup grated cheese

Layer Doritos on the bottom of a deep baking dish. Layer chopped chicken on top of Doritos. Mix Rotel and soups together and pour half over chicken. Spread grated cheese on top of soup. Repeat the layers and bake at 350 degrees for 30 - 40 minutes.

OVEN BAKED CHICKEN

8   chicken breasts
2   10 ¾ ounce cans cream of chicken soup
½   cup grated Parmesan cheese

Place chicken in single layer in jelly roll pan. Blend soup and cheese in bowl; spread evenly over chicken. Bake in pre-heated oven at 350 degrees for 1 hour and 15 minutes or until chicken is tender and brown. Remove chicken to platter; spoon sauce over chicken.

PEPPER CHICKEN

6-8 chicken breasts
¼   cup soy sauce
½   teaspoon salt
1   8 ounce can water chestnuts, drained and sliced
1   large green bell pepper cut into 1 inch pieces
2   tablespoons cornstarch

Remove skin from chicken. Place chicken in crock pot. Combine soy sauce, and 1 tablespoon water, pour over chicken. Sprinkle with salt. Cover and cook in crock pot on high for 1 hour 30 minutes. Scatter water chestnuts and green pepper slices on chicken and cook for 30 minutes more. Combine cornstarch and 2 tablespoons water and stir into liquid in crock pot. Cook stirring constantly until mixture thickens. Serve with rice.

RITZY CHICKEN BAKE

2   sticks butter, melted
8   chicken breasts
1½ sleeves Ritz Crackers

Crush Ritz crackers into very small pieces. Dip chicken in melted butter, and then dip in Ritz cracker crumbs. Place in baking dish. Sprinkle with salt. Bake covered for 45 minutes at 425 degrees. Remove cover and bake 15 more minutes.

SOUTHWEST CHICKEN CASSEROLE

4   chicken breasts, cooked and cut up
2   tablespoons olive oil
3   cloves garlic, minced
1   14 ounce can diced tomatoes
1   tablespoon red wine vinegar
½   teaspoon dried oregano
¼   teaspoon salt
¼   teaspoon pepper
1   15 ounce can black beans, drained and rinsed
1   4 ounce package Monterey Jack cheese, shredded
1   4 ounce package Cheddar cheese, shredded

Sauté garlic in olive oil. Stir in tomatoes, red wine vinegar, and all seasonings. Cover and simmer 5 minutes. Add black beans and cook 5 minutes more. Layer chicken in medium casserole dish. Top with black bean mixture, cover with cheeses. Cover and bake at 350 degrees for 30 minutes.

STIR-FRY CHICKEN AND BROCCOLI

1   pound chicken breast strips
2   tablespoons oil
4   cups vegetables, broccoli florets, pepper strips, sliced water chestnuts
1½ cups chicken broth
3   tablespoons soy sauce
2   tablespoons cornstarch
2   teaspoons brown sugar
1   teaspoon garlic powder
¾   teaspoon ground ginger
1½ cups Original Minute Rice

Stir fry chicken in hot oil in large skillet until browned. Add broccoli, pepper and water chestnuts; stir fry until crisp tender. Mix broth, soy sauce, cornstarch, sugar, garlic powder and ginger, add to skillet. Bring to boil for one minute. Meanwhile, prepare rice as directed on package. Serve chicken and vegetables over rice. Makes 4 servings.

TASTY CHICKEN LIVERS

3   tablespoons butter
2   large onions, sliced
2   large bell peppers, chopped
1   pound chicken livers
½   cup chili sauce
1   teaspoon lemon juice

In 12 inch skillet, over medium-high heat, in hot butter, cook onions and bell peppers 10 minutes, stirring occasionally. Meanwhile, trim membrane from livers. Add livers to onions and peppers in skillet. Cook until browned on all sides, about 5 minutes, stirring occasionally. Stir in chili sauce and lemon juice. Reduce heat to low and simmer 10 minutes, stirring occasionally. Serve over rice.

PORK

BREAKFAST CASSEROLE

1½ pounds pork sausage, fry, drain, and crumble
4   cups water
1   cup grits
½   stick butter
¼   pound sharp Cheddar cheese
3   eggs, beaten
½   cup milk

> Cook grits in the 4 cups of water. Add other ingredients and mix well. Spray casserole dish. Pour mixture into casserole dish. Bake at 400 degrees for 45 minutes. Vary by Oscar Mayer Real Bacon Bits. Can also vary with kind of cheese.

CAMP FIRE PORK CHOPS

4   pork loin chops
4   medium potatoes, quartered
1   large onion, sliced
1   14 ounce can Mexican tomatoes
¼   cup Worcestershire sauce
Goya seasoning

> Salt, pepper and Goya seasoning to taste. Place all ingredients inside foil. Cut slits in top of foil for steam to escape. Bake at 350 degrees for 1 and ½ hours, or until potatoes and chops are tender.

PORK CHOP CASSEROLE

6-8 pork chops
1 cup sour cream
1 10 ¾ ounce can cream of mushroom soup
6-8 medium potatoes, sliced
2 medium onions, sliced
salt to taste

Brown pork chops in skillet. Mix sour cream and soup. In a greased casserole put a layer of sliced potatoes, sprinkle with salt; add a layer of sliced onions and cover with sour cream sauce. Repeat. Place pork chops on top. Cover and bake at 350 degrees for 90 minutes.

PORK CHOP SPECIAL

6-8 center cut pork chops
1 cup Worcestershire sauce
3 tablespoons butter, melted
¼ cup A-1 sauce
juice of 1 lemon
½ teaspoon Tabasco

Arrange pork chops in a 9 x 13 inch casserole dish. Mix together other ingredients and pour over chops. Cover and bake at 300 degrees for 1 hour or until chops are tender.

PORK CHOPS ITALIANO

6 loin pork chops
salt and pepper to taste
1½ tablespoons vegetable oil
1 can sliced mushrooms or fresh mushrooms
1 medium onion, chopped
1 small clove garlic, crushed
2 medium bell peppers, cut into thin strips
3 8 ounce cans tomato sauce
1 teaspoon oregano
2 tablespoons lemon juice
½ cup dry sherry

Sprinkle pork chops with salt and pepper and brown on both sides in hot oil. Place chops in a shallow 2 quart baking dish; cover with mushrooms and set aside. Add onion, garlic and bell pepper to skillet; cook until tender. Add remaining ingredients and simmer for 5 minutes, pour over chops. Cover and bake at 350 degrees for 30 minutes. Remove cover and bake another 30 minutes.

QUICK AND EASY QUICHE LORRAINE

1   cup cream
4   egg yolks
pinch salt, pepper, and nutmeg
1   pound bacon or cubed ham
¼   pound mild Cheddar cheese, grated
¼   pound sharp Cheddar cheese, grated

Blend together cream, egg yolks, salt, pepper, and nutmeg. Set aside. Fry bacon until crisp and drain on paper towel. Fill prepared quiche shell or regular pie shell with over lapping layers of cheese and broken bacon. Pour blended ingredients over cheese and bacon. Bake at 375 degrees for 35 - 45 minutes until custard is puffed and crust is nicely browned.

TANGY AND SWEET PORK CHOPS

2   tablespoons salad oil

6¾   inch thick pork chops

1½   cups orange juice

3   tablespoons light brown sugar

1   tablespoon cornstarch

1½   teaspoons grated orange peel, optional

1½   teaspoons salt

⅛   teaspoon ground cloves

3   tablespoons Worcestershire sauce

3   tablespoons water

2¼   teaspoons cider vinegar

1   medium orange peeled and cut into sections, optional

Preheat oven to 350 degrees. In a large skillet heat oil until hot. Add pork chops, 3 at a time; brown on all sides. Arrange chops in a 3 quart baking dish. In a small saucepan combine orange juice, brown sugar, cornstarch, orange peel, salt, cloves, Worcestershire sauce, water, and vinegar, bring to a boil. Pour over pork chops. Bake covered for 25 minutes. Add orange sections and cook until pork chops are tender, about 5 minutes longer. Serve with buttered noodles or rice.

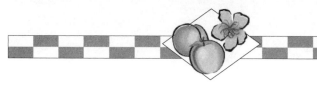

SEAFOOD

BAKED SALMON PATTIES

2	cups salmon, un-drained	½	cup mayonnaise
1	tablespoon chopped onion	½	cup chopped celery
¼	cup chopped green bell pepper	1	tablespoon Worcestershire sauce
1	cup saltine cracker crumbs	¼	teaspoon salt

Mix together and form patties. Place on greased cookie sheet. Bake at 425 degrees for 20 minutes or until brown.

CREOLE SHRIMP IN RICE RING

2	pounds fresh shrimp	1	large onion, chopped
1	clove garlic, minced	4	stalks celery, chopped
2	tablespoons salad oil	3 ½	cups tomatoes
salt and pepper to taste		2	bay leaves
1	pinch thyme		dash Tabasco sauce
2	cups rice		

Cook shrimp, clean and devein. Brown onion, garlic and celery in hot salad oil; add tomatoes, seasonings and Tabasco sauce. Cook 10 minutes. Add shrimp and cook 10 minutes more. Cook rice according to directions. Serve shrimp over rice.

SALMON STEW

1   16 ounce can red salmon
1   32 ounce carton milk
¼   cup butter
salt and pepper to taste

Remove bones and dark skin from salmon, drain. Melt butter; add milk, salmon, salt, and pepper. Heat thoroughly on medium heat. Serve with saltines or oyster crackers.

SHRIMP CASSEROLE

2   cups cooked rice
1   10 ounce can cream of mushroom soup
2   tablespoons butter, melted
1   tablespoon lemon juice
½   teaspoon pepper
1   pound raw shelled shrimp
1   cup Cheddar cheese cubes
2   tablespoons onion, chopped
½   teaspoon Worcestershire sauce

Mix well and bake in 375 degree oven for 45 minutes.

BREADS
and
ROLLS

Index

BANANA OATMEAL MUFFINS

1   cup sifted all purpose flour
½   cup sugar
2   teaspoons baking powder
½   teaspoon soda
½   teaspoon salt
⅔   cup rolled oats
¼   cup finely chopped nuts
1   egg
½   cup milk
2   tablespoons oil
½   cup well mashed bananas

Stir together the flour, sugar, baking powder, soda, and salt. Stir
in oats and nuts. In small bowl, beat egg slightly: add milk and
beat. Stir in oil and bananas: add this to dry ingredients. Fill
greased muffin tins ⅔ full and bake at 425 degrees for about 15
minutes. Yields: 1 dozen.

BISCUITS

2   cups self rising flour
⅓   cup Crisco
1   cup buttermilk

Sift flour into mixing bowl. Cut in Crisco with pastry cutter.
Mix in buttermilk with large spoon. Turn onto floured surface.
Pat to desired thickness and cut dough with biscuit cutter. Bake
on lightly greased pan for 15 minutes at 425 degrees or until
lightly brown.

CHEDDAR GARLIC BISCUITS

1 cup Bisquick
1 cup self rising flour
½ cup grated Cheddar cheese
⅔ cup buttermilk
4 tablespoons melted butter
¼ teaspoon garlic powder
½ teaspoon dill weed

Heat oven to 450 degrees. Mix Bisquick mix, flour, grated cheese and milk to form soft dough. Drop by spoonfuls onto ungreased cookie sheet. Brush with ½ garlic and dill butter. Bake at 450 degrees for 10-12 minutes. Remove for oven and brush with remaining garlic and dill butter.

CHICKEN PUFFS

1 stick margarine
1 cup water
¼ level teaspoon salt
1 cup sifted all purpose flour
4 eggs
1 cup Cheddar cheese, grated, optional

In a 2 quart saucepan, combine margarine, water and salt. Slowly bring to boiling, stirring occasionally, remove from heat: beat in flour and return to low heat. Stir vigorously until mixture forms a ball that doesn't separate. Remove from heat: add eggs one at a time and beat until smooth and shiny. Stir in cheese if desired. Drop dough onto greased baking sheet, using 1 level teaspoon for each puff. Bake at 400 degrees about 20 minutes. Remove from oven: cool and split. Stuff with chicken salad. They are also delicious stuffed with shrimp salad.

COFFEE CAKE MUFFINS

1½ cups sifted all purpose flour
½   cup granulated sugar
2   tablespoons baking powder
½   teaspoon salt
¼   cup shortening
1   egg, well beaten
½   cup milk

> Sift flour, sugar, baking powder and salt into mixing bowl. Cut in shortening until mixture resembles coarse crumbs. Mix egg and milk: add to flour mixture and stir until just moistened. Place half of batter into greased muffin tin. Sprinkle with nut mixture, below over batter and top with remaining batter. Bake at 350 degrees for approximately 20 minutes.

Topping

½   cup brown sugar
¼   cup chopped walnuts or pecans
1   tablespoon all purpose flour
1   teaspoon ground cinnamon
1   tablespoon butter, melted

> Combine all ingredients. Sprinkle on top of muffin mixture.

GOLDEN CORN FRITTERS

1   15 ounce can cream style golden corn
2½ cups Bisquick
½   teaspoon salt
2   tablespoons corn meal
1   tablespoon butter, melted

> Mix dry ingredients and add to melted butter and corn. Beat well and drop by spoonfuls in hot oil until browned.

HUSHPUPPIES

1   cup plain corn meal
4   teaspoons baking powder
1   cup self rising flour
½   teaspoon salt
½   cup chopped onions
4   tablespoons hot oil
1   cup whole kernel corn, optional
2   eggs, beaten

> Mix together and drop by spoon into hot oil until browned. Drain on paper towels and serve.

HUSHPUPPIES - FAVORITE

2   cups sifted corn meal, plain
1   cup sifted all purpose flour
1   teaspoon baking powder
½   teaspoon salt
½   teaspoon sugar
1   tablespoon melted butter
½   cup chopped onion
½   cup milk
¾   cup water
1   egg

> Mix all dry ingredients together. Add onions, then milk, water, butter and last the egg. Roll in balls ¾ inch thick. Fry in hot oil for 5-7 minutes. Yields: 8-10 servings.

HUSHPUPPIES - SIMPLY GOOD

1   cup self rising white cornmeal mix
½   cup dry onions
½   cup self rising flour
1   tablespoon sugar
1   large egg, lightly beaten
½   cup milk or beer
vegetable oil

> Combine first 4 ingredients, in a large bowl. Add egg and milk or beer to dry ingredients, stirring just until moistened. Let stand 10 minutes, Drop batter by rounded tablespoon into hot oil, 375 degrees, until browned. Drain on paper towels and serve.

INSTANT MIRACLE ROLLS

5	cups sifted self rising flour	3	packages yeast
¼	cup sugar	½	cup warm water
1	teaspoon soda	2	cups lukewarm buttermilk
1	cup Crisco		

Dissolve yeast in warm water and set aside. Blend flour, sugar, soda and Crisco together until it resembles coarse meal. Add yeast mixture and buttermilk. Mix together well. Fill greased muffin tins ½ full and bake at 400 degrees 15-20 minutes. For a fancier roll, roll dough into small balls and place three balls in each muffin tin. Unused dough will keep in refrigerator for 7-10 days.

JALAPENO CORNBREAD

3	cups self rising cornmeal	½	cup very finely chopped
2½	cups buttermilk		Jalapeño peppers
½	cup salad oil	1½	cup sharp cheese, grated
3	eggs, beaten	¼	pound bacon, cooked and
1	medium onion, grated		crumbled
2	tablespoons sugar	¼	cup chopped pimentos
1	cup cream style corn	½	clove garlic, crushed

Put cornmeal mix in large bowl: add milk and stir. Add other ingredients in order given. Bake at 400 degrees in greased muffin tins for approximately 20 minutes or until done.

JAM MUFFINS

2¼ cups all purpose flour
½ cup firmly packed brown sugar
1 tablespoon baking powder
½ teaspoon ground cinnamon
1 cup milk
1 cup fruit jam
¼ cup butter, softened
2 eggs, beaten

Combine flour, sugar, baking powder and cinnamon: make a well in center of mixture. Combine milk, jam, butter and eggs stirring well. Add to dry ingredients stirring just until moistened. Fill greased muffin tins ⅔ full. Bake at 350 degrees for 25 minutes or until brown. Yields: 2 dozen.

MAGIC ROLLS

4 cups Bisquick mix
¼ cup sugar
¼ cup butter, melted
2 eggs, beaten
1½ cups milk

Combine all ingredients in a medium mixing bowl, stirring until just moistened. Spoon batter into greased muffin tins, filling ½ full. Bake at 400 degrees for 15-20 minutes.

MAYONNAISE BISCUITS

1   cup self rising flour
2   tablespoons mayonnaise
⅔   cup milk

> Mix and drop into greased muffin tins. Bake at 450 degrees for approximately 15 minutes.

OLD FASHION BISCUITS

4   cups self rising flour sifted
¾   cup Crisco, melted
1¼ cups buttermilk

> Sift flour into a mixing bowl. Make a well into center of flour. Pour melted Crisco and buttermilk into well. Stir flour into Crisco and buttermilk. Work flour in until you have a soft dough formed. Pinch off and roll into balls. Place on greased cookie sheet. Press down with finger tips. Bake at 450 degrees for 10-12 minutes, or until browned.

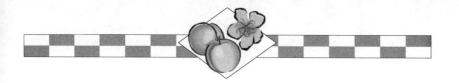

REFRIGERATOR BISCUITS

1   8 ounce package cream cheese, softened
½   cup butter
1   cup self rising flour

Beat cream cheese and butter at medium speed of mixer for 2 minutes or until mixture is creamy. Gradually add flour, beating at low speed just until blended. Spoon dough into miniature muffin pans, filling ⅔ full. Bake at 400 degrees for 17 minutes or until golden brown. Yields: 2 dozen. Dough can be refrigerated for up to 3 days.

SOUR CREAM "BISQUICKS"

2   cup Bisquick
1   stick real butter, melted
1   8 ounce carton sour cream

Mix well and drop in greased muffin tins. Use the tiny muffin tins: they are not good baked in the large ones. Bake at 400 degrees until brown.

SOUTHERN CORN BREAD

3	cups self rising corn meal	1½	cups self rising flour
1	egg, beaten	¾	cup shortening, melted
3	cups buttermilk	1	teaspoon salt

Mix all ingredients together. Pour into greased muffin tins, filling ½ full or use a 9 x 13 inch baking pan. Bake at 450 degrees for 20 - 30 minutes, or until brown.

SOUTHERN CORNBREAD DRESSING

½	gallon whole buttermilk	3	pounds plain meal
1	cup self rising flour	8	eggs
¾	cup Crisco		salt to taste

Mix together and bake at 400 degrees until brown.

PART 2

2	medium onions chopped fine	1	cup celery chopped fine
3	cans Swanson chicken broth	1	can cream of celery soup
1	can cream of chicken soup		

Crumble cooked corn bread until fine. Add onions and celery. Mix soup and broth with cornbread mixture. Place in a 9 x 13 inch buttered baking dish. Bake at 400 degrees until browned. Yields: 2, 9 x 13 inch pans.

SPOON ROLLS

1   package dry yeast
2   cups very warm water
1½ sticks butter, melted
¼   cup sugar
1   egg
4   cups self rising flour

> Dissolve yeast in 2 cups warm water. Melt butter: cream with sugar in a large bowl, then add beaten egg. Add dissolved yeast to creamed mixture. Then add the flour and stir until well mixed. Place in airtight bowl and keep in refrigerator. To cook, drop by spoonfuls into well greased muffin tins and bake at 350 degrees about 20 minutes or until browned. This dough keeps for several days.

SWEET POTATO BISCUITS

4   cups all purpose flour
2   tablespoons baking powder
2   teaspoons salt
1   cup butter
1   cup cooked mashed sweet potatoes
¾ -1 cup buttermilk

> Mix all ingredients together, roll out and bake on greased pan at 450 degrees for 10 -12 minutes or until browned.

YAM MUFFINS

1¾ cups all purpose flour

½ cup chopped pecans

¼ cup firmly packed brown sugar

1 tablespoon baking powder

2 teaspoons ground cinnamon

1 teaspoon salt

2 eggs, well beaten

1½ cups mashed yams

¾ cup milk

¼ cup butter, melted

ground cinnamon and sugar

Combine first 6 ingredients. Make a well in center of mixture. Combine eggs, yams, milk, and butter, add to dry ingredients stirring just until moistened. Spoon into greased muffin tins filling ⅔ full. Sprinkle with cinnamon and sugar. Bake at 425 degrees for 35 minutes. Yields: 1 ½ dozen.

DESSERTS

Index

APPLE CRISP

1 can sliced apples
½ cup dark brown sugar
1 cup chopped nuts
½ box white cake mix
1 stick butter, melted

Grease a 12 x 12 inch dish. Sprinkle sugar over apples and sprinkle cake mix over sugar. Cover with nuts. Pour butter over all. Bake 50 minutes at 350 degrees.

APPLE DUMPLINGS

4 small Granny Smith apples
1 package crescent rolls
1 cup orange juice
⅔ cup sugar
1 stick butter
cinnamon

Peel and core apples. Cut in fourths. Wrap in crescents and place in greased a 9 x 13 inch baking dish. Combine orange juice, sugar and butter. Bring to a boil. Pour over rolls and sprinkle with cinnamon and sugar. Bake at 350 degrees for 25 minutes.

BANANA PUDDING

6   egg yolks

1   cup sugar

6   tablespoons flour

2   cups evaporated milk

2   cups homogenized milk

1   teaspoon vanilla

4   bananas, sliced

3   dozen vanilla wafers

> Beat together, very well, egg yolks, sugar and flour. Add milk. Cook in microwave for 10 - 12 minutes, until smooth and thick, stirring every 2 minutes. Add vanilla. Pour over vanilla wafers and sliced bananas already arranged in a casserole dish.

BANANAS FLAMBÉ

½   cup butter

1   teaspoon cinnamon

⅓   cup dark rum

⅔   cup brown sugar

4   bananas, peeled and sliced

vanilla ice cream

> In saucepan heat butter, cinnamon and sugar until mixture is bubbly. Stir constantly. Add banana slices, heat thoroughly 2 - 3 minutes. In small pan, heat rum until warm, slowly pour over bananas and sauce. Do not stir. Ignite immediately and spoon over dishes of ice cream. Yields: 6 - 8 servings.

BLACKBERRY COBBLER

3 cups blackberries

white sandwich bread de-crusted

1 egg, beaten

2 cups sugar

2 teaspoons flour

1 stick butter, melted

Place blackberries in bottom of a buttered 9 x 9 inch baking dish. Cut crust from bread, cut each slice into 3 strips: place on top of blackberries, completely covering blackberries. Melt butter and mix with sugar and flour. Add egg and mix well. Drizzle over bread. Bake at 350 degrees for 30 - 35 minutes or until brown.

BLUEBERRY CHEESE CAKE

1½ cups Graham cracker crumbs

½ stick butter

¾ cup sugar

Mix and press into a 9 x 13 inch pan.

PART 2

2 eggs

2 8 ounce packages cream cheese

1 cup sugar

1 teaspoon vanilla

blueberry pie filling

Mix eggs, cream cheese, sugar and vanilla together. Pour on top of pie crust. Bake 15 minutes at 375 degrees. When cool, place 1 large can blueberry pie filling on top. Cut into squares and serve.

BLUEBERRY COBBLER

¼   cup butter
⅔   cup milk
1½ cups biscuit mix
1   cup sugar
1   can blueberry pie filling

> Heat oven to 400 degrees. Melt butter in an 11 x 17 inch baking dish. Mix milk, biscuit mix and sugar, stir until smooth, and pour over butter. Drop spoonfuls of filling over batter that has been placed in baking dish. Bake 30 - 35 minutes until deep golden brown. Batter will rise to the top as cobbler bakes forming a cake like crust.

BLUEBERRY CRUNCH

1   large can crushed pineapple, un-drained
2-3 cups fresh blueberries
½   cup sugar, divided
1   box yellow cake mix
1   cup butter, melted
1   cup chopped pecans

> Place in order given into a 9 x 13 inch baking dish. Sprinkle the remaining ¼ cup sugar over the top. Bake at 325 degrees for 25 - 40 minutes.

BLUEBERRY DELIGHT

2   cups Graham cracker crumbs
½   cup butter, melted
½   cup sugar

Mix together and press half of crumb mixture into a 9 x 12 inch baking dish.

FILLING

1   8 ounce package cream cheese
1   large package Dream Whip
1   cup sugar
1   can blueberry pie filling

Cream sugar and cream cheese. Whip Dream Whip by directions on package, until stiff. Fold sugar and cream cheese mixture into Dream Whip. Place a layer of this in pie crust, than a layer of blueberry pie filling. Top with rest of Dream Whip mixture. Sprinkle with other half of cracker crumbs.

BUTTER - ROLL

2   cans Pillsbury crescent rolls

1   stick butter

1   quart milk

1½ cups sugar

nutmeg

½   cup sugar

Separate rolls into 8 triangles. Put 1 square of butter on large end of roll. Sprinkle with nutmeg and sugar from the ½ cup of sugar. Roll triangles up in crescents. Place in long baking dish 13 x 9 x 2 inches. Mix the milk and the 1 ½ cups sugar together. Pour into baking dish. Do not pour over top of rolls. Bake at 400 degrees until rolls are browned. Serve warm.

CAKE DOUGHNUTS

1   cup + 2 tablespoons sugar
1½ tablespoons butter, softened
3   eggs
½   cup sour cream
½   cup buttermilk
6   cups all purpose flour, measured before sifting
2   teaspoons baking powder
1   teaspoon baking soda
1   teaspoon cinnamon
1   teaspoon nutmeg
1   teaspoon salt
salad oil
powdered sugar

Cream butter, sugar and eggs until light and fluffy. Add sour cream and buttermilk mixing well. Combine flour, baking powder, soda, spices, and salt and add to egg mixture beating until smooth. Chill dough 30 minutes. Roll out to 3/8 inch thickness on a lightly floured surface. Cut with a floured doughnut cutter. Heat 3 - 4 inches of oil to 375 degrees, drop in 3 or 4 doughnuts at a time. Cook about 1 minute or until golden brown on one side. Turn as doughnut rises to surface and cook on other side about 1 minute. Drain on absorbent towels. Dust with powdered sugar while warm. Yields: about 3 dozen.

CHEESE CAKE

2	3 ounce packages cream cheese	1	8 ounce carton sour cream
½	cup sugar	8	teaspoons sugar
2	eggs	¼	teaspoon vanilla
1	teaspoon vanilla	1	Graham cracker pie crust

Cream cheese and ½ cup sugar together: beat in eggs and add vanilla. Place in Graham cracker crust. Bake at 350 degrees for 20 minutes. Cool 5 minutes. Mix sour cream, 8 teaspoons sugar and vanilla. Spread on top of filling and bake 5 minutes. Cool. Place in refrigerator. Serve plain or top with your favorite pie filling.

CHERRY YUM - YUM

2	cups Graham cracker crumbs	1	8 ounce package cream cheese, softened
½	cup melted butter	¾	cup sugar
½	cup sugar	½	teaspoon vanilla
2	envelopes Dream Whip	1	can cherry pie filling

Mix together Graham cracker crumbs, melted butter and ½ cup sugar. Press half of crumb mixture into a 9 x 12 inch dish. Prepare Dream Whip according to package directions. Mix other ingredients together well and blend into Dream Whip mixture. Pour into dish and sprinkle the other half of crumb mixture over top. Spread cherry pie filling over this. Chill 1 hour before serving. Keep refrigerated.

CHOCOLATE DESSERT FONDUE

3   3 ounce packages baking chocolate
3   tablespoons whipping cream
2   tablespoons kirsch or brandy
1   pinch cinnamon
½   tablespoon instant coffee

Dissolve chocolate in fondue pot. Add other ingredients and stir until creamy. Keep on very low alcohol or sterno flame. Dippers for Chocolate Fondue: strawberries and bananas, cut into chunks, apples cut into chunks, grapes, Maraschino cherries, and orange sections.

CREAM CHEESE DANISH

2   packages crescent rolls
1   8 ounce package cream cheese
1   cup sugar
1   teaspoon vanilla

Cream together, cream cheese, sugar and vanilla. Spray a 9 x 13 inch baking pan with Pam. Press 1 can crescent rolls into bottom of pan. Pour cream cheese mixture on top. Press on next can of crescent rolls. Sprinkle ½ cup of sugar on top layer. Bake at 350 until brown. Cut in squares.

DATE PUDDING

1   cup all purpose flour
¾   cup packed light brown sugar
1   teaspoon baking powder
½   cup milk
1   cup chopped pitted dates
1¼ cups boiling water
1   cup chopped pecans or walnuts
¾   cup packed light brown sugar
1   tablespoon butter
1   teaspoon vanilla

>   Grease a 2 quart baking dish. In mixing bowl stir together flour,
>   ¾ cup brown sugar, and baking powder. Add milk, mix well. Stir
>   in the chopped dates: spread the batter in the baking dish. In
>   a medium bowl, stir together boiling water, pecans or walnuts,
>   the remaining ¾ cup brown sugar, butter and vanilla: pour over
>   the date mixture in the baking dish. Bake, uncovered in a 350
>   degree oven for about 30 minutes or until set. Serve warm with
>   unsweetened whipped cream.

DELICIOUS CHEESECAKE

2   eggs
2   8 ounce packages cream cheese
1   cup sugar
1   teaspoon vanilla
1   Graham cracker pie crust

>   Cream together well. Pour into a Graham cracker pie crust and
>   bake at 375 for 30 minutes or until set. Spread favorite pie filling
>   on top, blueberry or cherry.

DELICIOUS PINEAPPLE PUDDING

2 tablespoons butter

1½ cups sugar

3 tablespoons all purpose flour

pinch salt

3 eggs, beaten

1¼ cups evaporated milk

1 8 ounce can crushed pineapple, un-drained

1 teaspoon vanilla extract

1 cup chopped pecans or walnuts, optional

4 dozen vanilla wafers

Melt butter in saucepan. Stir in sugar, flour and salt. Add eggs and milk, stirring, until thickened. Remove from heat and stir in pineapple, vanilla and nuts. Cool. Line bottom and sides of a 1 ½ quart casserole dish with vanilla wafers. Spoon in half of pudding. Top with a layer of vanilla wafers and remaining pudding. Top with whipped cream if desired.

DO NOTHING CAKE

2   cups flour
2   cups sugar
2   eggs
1   teaspoon vanilla extract
½   teaspoon salt
1   teaspoon baking soda
1   large can crushed pineapple, un-drained

Mix all ingredients well by hand. Pour batter into a greased 9 x 13 inch pan. Bake at 350 degrees for 30 minutes.

Frosting

1   stick margarine
1   cup sugar
⅔   cup evaporated milk
1   cup chopped nuts
1   cup coconut

Mix margarine, sugar and milk in saucepan. Simmer for 5 minutes. Add nuts and coconut. Pour frosting over hot cake. Let cake stand until completely cool. Cut into squares.

FAIRY GINGERBREAD

1 cup sugar

½ cup butter

2 eggs

1 cup milk

1 cup molasses

2½ cups plain flour

½ teaspoon baking soda

1 tablespoon powdered ginger

Cream sugar and butter together. Beat in eggs. Add milk and molasses. Sift flour, baking soda, and ginger into mixture, beating well. Bake in a jelly roll pan at 350 degrees for 30 - 45 minutes.

FOUR LAYER DELIGHT

1ST LAYER CRUST

1   cup all purpose flour
1   stick butter, softened
1   cup chopped nuts

> Mix and pat into an 8 x 12 or 10 inch square baking dish. Bake at 350 degrees for 25 minutes. Cool completely.

2ND LAYER

1   3 ounce package cream cheese, softened
1   cup powdered sugar
1   teaspoon vanilla
1   cup Cool Whip

> Beat first 3 ingredients together and fold in Cool Whip. Spread over cooled crust.

3RD LAYER

1   5 ounce package instant chocolate pudding
2   cups milk
1   teaspoon vanilla

> Mix together and spread over second layer.

4TH LAYER

chopped nuts or shaved chocolate
Cool Whip

> Cover third layer with thin layer of Cool Whip and garnish with chopped nuts or shaved chocolate. Refrigerate and serve cold.

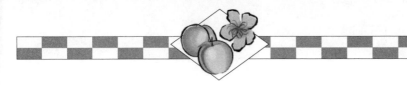

GELATIN RIBBON LOAF

1   3 ounce package lime Jello
1   3 ounce package raspberry Jello
1   15 ounce jar applesauce
18 double Graham crackers
1   envelope Dream Whip
3   tablespoons 10 X sugar
¼   teaspoon almond extract

Place lime and raspberry gelatin in separate bowls: add ¾ cup applesauce to each flavor and stir until thoroughly blended. Place 2 double crackers end to end, on a platter: spread with ½ cup lime mixture. Repeat layers, ending with crackers. Prepare whipped topping mix as directed on package, omitting the vanilla and adding 10 X sugar and almond extract before beating. Spread over top and sides of loaf. Chill and serve.

OLD FASHION RICE PUDDING

4½ cups milk
¾   cup uncooked rice
1   large egg
½   cup sugar
2   teaspoons vanilla
½   teaspoon salt

Warm the milk in a medium size saucepan over medium low heat. Stir in rice. Bring to a simmer and cook, uncovered, stirring frequently until the rice is very tender. about 35 minutes. In a medium size bowl, whisk together the egg, sugar, vanilla and salt. Gradually stir in some of the rice mixture until well blended. Return the mixture to the sauce pan and stir over medium low heat for 1 minute to cook the egg. Pour the mixture into 6 custard cups and sprinkle with cinnamon. Refrigerate until chilled.

PARK AVENUE BARS

1   8 ounce package cream cheese, softened
1   box 10 X powdered sugar
1   box Pillsbury yellow cake mix with pudding in mix
3   eggs
1   stick butter
1   cup pecans, chopped fine
1   teaspoon vanilla

Mix cake mix, 1 egg, butter, and nuts. Press into a greased 9 x 13 inch baking dish. Combine cream cheese, 2 eggs, vanilla and 10 X sugar, beat until creamy. Spread over cake mixture. Bake at 325 degrees for 40 minutes or until golden brown on top. Cut into squares and serve.

PINA COLADA BREAD PUDDING

8   sandwich bread slices
2   3 ounce packages cream cheese softened
1   cup firmly packed light brown sugar
6   large eggs
1   cup milk
2   8 ounce cans crushed pineapple, drained
2   cups flaked coconut
Coconut Sauce

Trim crust from bread and discard. Cut bread into ½ inch cubes, and place on baking sheet. Bake at 375 degrees for 10 - 12 minutes or until toasted. Beat cream cheese at medium speed with mixer until smooth, add sugar, beating well. Add eggs, one at a time, beating until blended. Batter will be slightly lumpy. Stir in milk, pineapple and coconut, fold in bread cubes. Spoon into a lightly greased 1 ½ quart baking dish. Bake at 375 degrees for 30 minutes or until a knife inserted in center comes out clean. Serve with coconut sauce.

COCONUT SAUCE

1   cup cream of coconut
1   8 ounce carton sour cream

Pour cream of coconut through a wire mesh strainer into a small bowl. Whisk in sour cream. Serve over bread pudding.

PINEAPPLE CASSEROLE

2   cans pineapple tidbits
1   cup Cheddar cheese, grated
1   8 ounce package cream cheese
1   cup sugar
6   tablespoons pineapple juice
6   tablespoons flour
1½ packages Ritz crackers
1   stick butter

> Drain pineapple; combine with Cheddar cheese, set aside. Combine softened cream cheese with sugar, pineapple juice and flour. Mix with pineapple and Cheddar cheese mixture. Crush crackers and combine with melted butter, sprinkle on top of pineapple mixture. Bake at 350 degrees for 20 minutes or until hot and bubbly.

PINEAPPLE PUDDING

3   cups milk
3   eggs
1   cup sugar
1   teaspoon vanilla
4   tablespoons flour
1   can crushed pineapple, drained

> Drain pineapple. Mix all other ingredients in blender or with whisk. Put in bowl. Microwave 2 minutes. Stir this until mixture is thick like pudding. Add pineapple and refrigerate.

RICE PUDDING

2 cups cooked rice
1¼ cups sugar
2 cups milk
4 eggs, beaten
1 teaspoon vanilla
raisins, optional
nutmeg

> Mix all ingredients. Sprinkle nutmeg on top. Dot with butter.
> Bake at 350 degrees for 50 - 60 minutes.

SOUTHERN SWEET POTATO PIE

1½ cups sweet potatoes, cooked and mashed
1 cup sugar
2½ tablespoons butter, softened
⅔ cup evaporated milk
3 egg yolks, beaten
1 teaspoon vanilla extract
1 teaspoon nutmeg
3 egg whites
1 unbaked 9 inch deep dish pie shell

> Combine sweet potatoes, sugar and butter: stir well. Stir in
> milk, egg yolks, vanilla, and nutmeg, set aside. Beat egg whites,
> at room temperature at high speed with mixer until stiff peaks
> form. Fold egg whites into sweet potato mixture. Pour mixture
> into unbaked pastry shell. Bake at 375 degrees for 10 minutes:
> reduce heat to 350 degrees and bake 45 minutes or until set.

STRAWBERRY BOTTOM CHEESECAKE

1 6 ounce ready Graham cracker crust
1 4 ounce package cream cheese, softened
¼ cup sugar
½ cup sour cream
1 teaspoon vanilla
1 4 ounce carton frozen non dairy whipped topping, thawed
1 16 ounce package fresh strawberries, thinly sliced
1 cup strawberry glaze

Beat cream cheese until smooth. Gradually beat in sugar. Add sour cream and vanilla. Fold in whipping cream. Spread thin layer of glaze over bottom of crust. Place strawberry slices on glaze and cover with remaining glaze. Gently spoon cream cheese mixture over glazed strawberries. Cover with inverted dome and chill until set, at least 4 hours. Store pie in refrigerator.

STRAWBERRY BREAD

3 cups all purpose flour
1 tablespoons ground cinnamon
1 teaspoon baking soda
1 teaspoon salt
1¼ cups oil
3 large eggs
2 cups sugar
2 10 ounce packages frozen strawberries, thawed and drained
1 cup chopped pecans

Stir together dry ingredients. Set aside. Mix oil, eggs and sugar together. Add dry ingredients and stir until moistened. Stir in strawberries and pecans. Pour into two greased and floured loaf pans. Bake at 350 degrees for one hour or until a pick comes out clean. Cool loaves in pan for 10 minutes. Then turn out onto racks to cool. Yields: 2 loaves

STRAWBERRY DELIGHT

1   cup all purpose flour
¼   cup firmly packed brown sugar
½   cup chopped pecans
½   cup melted butter
1   10 ounce package frozen strawberries
1   cup sugar
2   egg whites
2   teaspoons fresh lemon juice
1   8 ounce carton whipping cream, whipped

Combine flour, brown sugar, pecans and butter. Pat into bottom of a 9 inch square pan and bake at 350 degrees for 20 minutes. Stir often. Let cool. Combine strawberries, sugar, lemon juice and egg whites: beat at high speed of mixer about 20 minutes or until light and fluffy. Fold whipped cream into mixture. Remove ⅓ of crumb mixture from pan - pat remaining crumbs into smooth layer. Pour mixture over crumbs in pan and sprinkle reserved crumbs on top: freeze. Yields: 8 - 10 servings.

STRAWBERRY PUDDING

2   3 ounce packages vanilla instant pudding mix
3   cups cold milk
1   3 ounce package strawberry Jello
1½   pints fresh or frozen sweetened strawberries
1   8 ounce carton sour cream
1   12 ounce carton Cool Whip
Vanilla Wafers

Beat the pudding and milk until thick. Heat strawberries and dry Jello until Jello is melted. Add sour cream to pudding mix. Fold in Cool Whip. In a 9 x 13 inch dish, place a layer of vanilla wafers, strawberries and pudding mix. Repeat layers. Serve.

STRAWBERRY TRIFLE

1   16 ounce carton Cool Whip
2   10 ounce packages
    frozen strawberries, thawed

1   can Eagle Brand
    condensed milk
1   sponge cake

Tear sponge cake into bite size pieces and place in glass serving bowl. Mix Cool Whip, condensed milk and strawberries. Pour over sponge cake. Mix well. Serve.

ZUCCHINI BREAD

4   eggs
1   cup cooking oil
3½ cups plain flour
1⅓ teaspoons baking soda
3   teaspoons cinnamon
½   cup chopped nuts

2¼ cups sugar
2   cups grated zucchini
1   teaspoon salt
1   teaspoon vanilla
¾   teaspoon baking powder
½   cup raisins, optional

Blend together eggs, sugar, oil, zucchini, and vanilla. Add flour, salt, soda, cinnamon, and baking powder. Mix well. Add chopped pecans and raisins. Blend well. Pour into greased tube or Bundt pan. Bake at 325 degrees for 1 hour and 15 minutes.

GLAZE TOPPING

½   cup powdered sugar
1   teaspoon milk

1   teaspoon lemon flavoring

Mix all ingredients, blending well. Pour over cake while hot.

PIES

BANANA CREAM PIE

2   3 ounce packages cream cheese
1   14 ounce can Eagle brand condensed milk
Juice from 3 lemons
1   teaspoon vanilla
3   bananas, sliced
Graham cracker pie crust

> Cream together well. Pour into a Graham pie crust which has been lined with sliced bananas. Chill and serve.

BANANA SPLIT PIE

1   Graham cracker pie crust
1   cup sugar
1   2 ounce package cream cheese, softened
2   bananas, sliced
1   medium crushed pineapple, drained well
1   8 ounce carton Cool Whip
chopped nuts
Maraschinos cherries, halved

> Cream the sugar with the cream cheese and spread in pie crust. Slice the bananas and spread over the cream cheese mixture. Spread pineapple over this. Cover with Cool Whip and sprinkle nuts and place halved cherries over top. Refrigerate until ready to serve.

BUTTERMILK PIE

1   cup sugar
1   cup buttermilk
dash salt
2   tablespoons flour
3   eggs, beaten
1   stick butter, melted
2   teaspoons vanilla

> Mix all ingredients together. Pour in deep dish pie shell. Bake at 350 degrees for 30 minutes or until set.

BUTTERNUT SQUASH PIE

1½   cups cooked squash
1¼   cups sugar
4   eggs, separated
½   stick butter, melted
1   cup evaporated milk
1   teaspoon lemon extract
nutmeg
1   unbaked deep dish pie shell

> Peel squash and remove seed. Cook sliced squash in salted water until tender: drain. Mix squash and sugar. Add well beaten egg yolks, butter and lemon extract. Beat well. Beat egg whites until stiff: fold into squash mixture. Pour in unbaked pie shell. Sprinkle top with nutmeg. Bake 40 - 45 minutes at 350 degrees or until set.

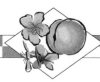

BUTTERSCOTCH PIE

½   cup sifted all purpose flour

1   cup brown sugar

¼   teaspoon salt

2   cups scalded milk, very hot

3   egg yolks, slightly beaten

3   tablespoons butter

1   teaspoon vanilla

Mix flour, sugar and salt, gradually add scalded milk. Cook over moderate heat, stirring constantly, until mixture thickens and boils. Cook 2 minutes and remove from heat. Add small amounts of hot mixture to egg yolks: then stir yolks into remaining hot mixture. Cook 1 minute, stirring constantly. Add butter and vanilla: cool slightly. Pour into baked deep dish pie shell. Note: This is easy to cook in microwave. Just remember to stir often.

MERINGUE

3   egg whites

¼   teaspoon cream of tartar

6   tablespoons sugar

Beat egg whites and cream of tartar until peaks form. Add sugar gradually and continue beating until stiff. Spread over pie and bake at 350 degrees until lightly browned.

CHERRY PIE WITH HOMEMADE PIE CRUST

3   cups self rising flour
1   cup Crisco

> Work together with a pastry blender or fork. Add ice cold water until it is consistency of biscuit dough. Knead with hands, add little flour if needed. Refrigerate overnight. Roll out on lightly floured board, place in lightly greased pie plate.

CHERRY FILLING

1   can cherry pie filling
1   tablespoon butter
⅓   cup light brown sugar

> Pour into crust. Top with second pie crust. Cut slits in top. Bake at 375 degrees for 10 minutes. Reduce oven temperature to 350 degrees. Bake until browned. About 10 minutes before done, run butter over top of crust. Sprinkle with sugar.

CHERRY-O-CREAM CHEESE PIE

1   8 ounce package cream cheese, softened
1   14 ounce can Eagle Brand sweetened condensed milk
⅓   cup lemon juice
1   teaspoon vanilla
1   15 ounce can cherry pie filling
1   Graham cracker pie crust

Beat cream cheese until light and fluffy. Gradually add condensed milk and mix well. Blend in lemon juice and vanilla. Pour into Graham cracker pie crust. Spread cherry pie filling over top. Chill and serve.

CHOCOLATE CHESS PIE

1   cup sugar
3   tablespoons corn meal
2½ tablespoons cocoa
½   cup Karo syrup
3   eggs
1   stick butter
1   teaspoon vanilla
1   cup chopped pecans
1   cup flaked coconut
1   unbaked deep dish pie shell

Mix all ingredients together, pour into the pie shell. Bake at 325 degrees for 45 - 50 minutes or until set.

CHOCOLATE CREAM PIE

2	squares baking chocolate
2	tablespoons butter
⅓	cup flour
1	cup sugar
¼	teaspoon salt
2½	cups scalded milk, very hot
3	eggs, separated
¾	teaspoon vanilla

Melt chocolate and butter in top of double boiler. Mix flour, sugar, salt, and stir in chocolate. Add hot milk and stir constantly until mixture is fully thickened. Beat egg yolks well. Stir in a little of the chocolate mixture, then pour into rest of the hot mixture and cook 2 minutes stirring constantly. Remove from heat, stir in vanilla. Pour into baked deep dish pie shell. Note: This can be cooked in the microwave.

MERINGUE

3	egg whites
6	tablespoons sugar
¼	teaspoon cream of tartar

Beat whites and cream of tartar until peaks form: add sugar 1 tablespoon at a time. Continue beating until stiff. Spread on pie. Bake at 350 degrees until browned.

CLASSIC CHESS PIE

1   unbaked deep dish pie crust
2   cups sugar
2   tablespoons cornmeal
1   tablespoon all purpose flour
¼   teaspoon salt
½   cup butter, melted
¼   cup milk
1   tablespoon white vinegar
½   teaspoon vanilla extract
4   large eggs, lightly beaten
nutmeg

Stir together sugar and next 7 ingredients until blended. Add eggs, stirring well. Pour filling into piecrust. Bake at 350 degrees for 50 - 55 minutes, shielding edges with aluminum foil after 10 minutes to prevent excessive browning. Cool completely on a wire rack.

COCONUT - PINEAPPLE PIE

4   eggs
1   tablespoon corn meal
1   8 ounce can crushed pineapple
2   cups sugar
1½ cups flaked coconut
½   stick butter
1   unbaked deep dish pie shell

Combine and mix all ingredients well. Pour into unbaked pie shell. Bake at 300 degrees for 30 - 40 minutes or until firm.

COCONUT CREAM PIE

¼   cup flour
½   cup sugar
¼   teaspoon salt
1½ cups scalded milk, very hot
3   eggs, separated
1   cup coconut
2   tablespoons butter
½   teaspoon vanilla

Mix flour, ½ cup sugar and salt in top of double boiler: add scalded milk and stir well. Cook until thick and smooth, stirring constantly. Beat egg yolks well, stir in a little of the hot mixture and pour back into double boiler. Cook about 2 more minutes stirring constantly. Remove from heat, add butter and vanilla. Pour into baked deep dish pie shell. Note: This can be cooked in the microwave.

MERINGUE

3   egg whites
6   tablespoons sugar
¼   teaspoon cream of tartar

Beat egg whites and cream of tartar until peaks form: add sugar a tablespoon at a time. Continue beating on high until stiff. Spread on pie and bake at 350 degrees until browned.

CREAM CHEESE PECAN PIE

1   8 ounce package cream cheese
⅓   cup sugar
1   teaspoon vanilla extract
1   egg, beaten

Mix all ingredients together. Pour into a deep dish pie shell.

TOPPING

1¼ cups chopped nuts
3   eggs, beaten
1   cup white Karo syrup
1   teaspoon vanilla extract
½   cup sugar

Sprinkle pie shell filling with the chopped nuts. Mix together remaining ingredients and pour over pecans. Bake at 350 degrees for 50 - 60 minutes.

CREAM CHEESE PUMPKIN PIE

1   3 ounce package cream cheese
1   cup + 1 tablespoon half & half milk
1   tablespoon sugar
1½ cups Cool Whip
1   Graham cracker pie crust
2   packages vanilla pudding
1   16 ounce can pumpkin
1   teaspoon cinnamon
½   teaspoon ginger
½   teaspoon ground cloves

Mix cream cheese, 1 tablespoon milk, and sugar until smooth. Stir in Cool Whip and pour into Graham cracker pie crust. Mix 1 cup milk and pudding, set aside. Mix pumpkin and all spices, combine with vanilla pudding mixture. Pour into pie crust. Refrigerate at least 2 hours.

CRUSTY COCONUT PIE

½   cup milk
1½ cups coconut
¼   cup butter
1   cup sugar
3   eggs
1   teaspoon vanilla
1   unbaked deep dish pie shell

Pour milk over coconut and set aside while creaming butter and sugar. Add eggs, and beat mixture well. Then add milk and coconut and vanilla flavoring. Pour into unbaked pie shell. Bake at 350 degrees for about 30 minutes or until pie is golden brown and firm.

DATE PECAN PIE

2   tablespoons butter, melted

¼   cup light cream

¾   cup sugar

2   tablespoons flour

1   teaspoon salt

2   eggs

1   cup dates, chopped

1   cup pecan halves

1   teaspoon vanilla

1   cup dark corn syrup

1   deep dish pie shell

Combine butter and cream. Mix together sugar, flour and salt, blend in cream mixture, add syrup, mix together and beat in eggs at medium speed. Stir in dates, pecans and vanilla. Pour into unbaked pastry shell. Bake at 400 degrees for 15 minutes: reduce heat to 350 degrees and continue cooking for 30 - 35 minutes longer or until pie is set. Filling should be slightly less set in center than at outer edge.

DELICIOUS PEACH PIE

1   cup sugar

⅓   cup butter

¾   cup flour

6   medium peaches, sliced

1   deep dish pie crust, unbaked

Mix sugar, butter and flour until crumbly. Line pie shell with ½ of this mixture. Place sliced peaches on top and place rest of flour mixture on top of peaches. Bake at 400 degrees for 15 minutes. Reduce heat to 350 degrees and bake for 45 minutes - 1 hour.

EASY BUTTERSCOTCH PIE

2   cans Eagle Brand condensed milk
Graham cracker pie crust
whipped cream
crushed chocolate toffee bars

Cook condensed milk in slow crock pot for 2 - 3 hours, stirring often, or until it turns the color of peanut butter. Pour into the Graham cracker pie crust. Serve with whipped cream. Garnish with crushed chocolate toffee bars.

EASY FRUIT PIE

¾   cup self rising flour
¾   cup milk
1   cup sugar
¾   stick butter
2   cups fruit
½   cup sugar

Mix flour, milk and 1 cup sugar together well. Melt ¾ stick butter in 8 inch square pan. Pour flour mixture over butter. Mix 2 cups fruit and ½ cup sugar together. Pour fruit over flour mixture and do not stir. Bake at 325 degrees for 1 hour.

EASY PIE

1   cup Graham cracker crumbs
3   egg whites
1   cup sugar
1   cup chopped nuts
1   teaspoon vanilla extract

Beat egg whites until stiff. Fold in remaining ingredients and pour into pie dish. Bake at 350 degrees for 20 minutes.

EASY PINEAPPLE PIE

¾   cup flour
¾   cup milk
1   cup sugar
1   stick melted butter
1   can crushed pineapple

Blend together flour, milk, sugar and butter. Pour into a 9 inch pie plate. Pour pineapple over batter. Bake at 325 degrees for 1 hour.

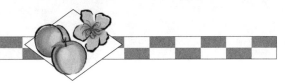

FAVORITE CHESS PIE

2   cups sugar
1   stick butter
4   eggs, beaten
2   tablespoons corn meal
¼   cup milk
1   teaspoon nutmeg
1   tablespoon plain flour

Mix all ingredients. Pour in unbaked deep dish pie shell. Bake at 350 degrees for 50 minutes. Sprinkle top with nutmeg.

FAVORITE LEMON PIE

2½ cups sugar
6   tablespoons flour
3   eggs, beaten
12 tablespoons butter, melted
1½ tablespoons lemon extract
1½ cups buttermilk
2   deep dish pie shells

Blend sugar and flour: add to eggs, then butter, lemon extract, and buttermilk. Stir well to mix. Pour into 2 unbaked pie shells. Bake at 350 degrees for 50 - 60 minutes or until custard sets and tops are browned.

FRESH STRAWBERRY PIE

1   cup water
1   cup sugar
3   tablespoons cornstarch
4-5 drops red food coloring
½   package strawberry Jello
1   24 ounce carton fresh strawberries
1   baked deep dish pie crust

> Mix together water, sugar and cornstarch: cook over medium heat until thick. Remove from heat and add Jello and food coloring. Pour over fresh strawberries. Spoon into baked pie shell. Chill and serve topped with whipped cream.

FROZEN LEMONADE PIE

1   14 ounce can Eagle Brand condensed milk
1   6 ounce can frozen lemonade thawed and undiluted
1   8 ounce carton Cool Whip
large Graham cracker pie crust

> Mix condensed milk, lemonade and Cool Whip together until smooth. Pour in Graham cracker pie crust. Garnish with lemon slices. Keep refrigerated.

GREAT FRUIT PIE

1½ cups Graham cracker crumbs
¾   cup sugar
¾   stick butter
1   can Eagle Brand condensed milk
1   8 ounce package cream cheese
1   can any flavor pie filling
chopped nuts (optional)

Mix together Graham cracker crumbs, sugar and butter. Pat into a 9 x 13 inch baking dish. Mix condensed milk and cream cheese: pour into Graham cracker crust. Pour large can of your favorite pie filling over top of cream cheese mixture. Sprinkle with nuts. Bake at 350 degrees for 20 - 30 minutes.

HAWAIIAN PIE

1   20 ounce can crushed pineapple with juice
6   tablespoons flour
1   cup sugar
1   6 ounce package frozen grated coconut
2   bananas, sliced
⅔   cup chopped pecans
1   8 ounce carton Cool Whip
2   9 inch baked pie shells

Mix sugar with flour: add to crushed pineapple. Cook until mixture thickens. Cool. Divide mixture into 2 pie shells. Add a layer of sliced banana, nuts, and coconut. Cover pie with Cool Whip. Chill and serve.

ICE BOX LEMON PIE

3   egg yolks
1   14 ounce can Eagle Brand condensed milk
Juice of 3 lemons
1   Graham cracker or vanilla wafer pie crust

Beat egg yolks: add condensed milk and lemon juice. Mix well. Pour into Graham cracker pie crust or a vanilla wafer pie crust.

MERINGUE

2   egg whites
¼   teaspoon cream of tartar
¼   cup sugar

Beat on high egg whites and cream of tartar until peaks begin to form, gradually add sugar and continue until stiff peaks. Spread over pie. Place in 350 degree oven until golden brown.

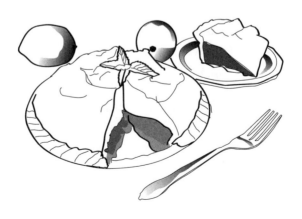

KAHLUA PECAN PIE

¼   cup butter
¾   cup sugar
1   teaspoon vanilla extract
2   tablespoons flour
3   eggs
½   cup Kahlua
½   cup dark corn syrup
¾   cup evaporated milk
1   cup whole or chopped pecans
½   cup heavy cream, whipped
1   unbaked deep dish pie crust

Cream together: butter, sugar, vanilla, and flour. Mix well. Beat in eggs one at a time. Stir in Kahlua, corn syrup, evaporated milk and pecans. Mix well. Pour into pie crust. Bake at 400 degrees for 10 minutes. Then reduce heat to 325 degrees and bake until firm: about 40 minutes. When ready to serve garnish with cream and pecan halves.

KEY LIME PIE

CRUST

16   Graham crackers, crushed

3   tablespoons sugar

1   stick butter

Mix the ingredients and press into a 9 inch pie plate. Bake in a preheated 350 degree oven for 10 - 12 minutes until lightly browned. Place on a rack to cool.

FILLING

4   large egg yolks

1   14 ounce can sweetened condensed milk

⅔   cup fresh key lime juice, approximately 12 key limes

2   tablespoons grated lime, green portion only

whipping cream for garnish, optional

Beat on medium with electric mixer and beat the egg yolks until they are thick and turn to a light yellow, don't over mix. Turn the mixer off and add the sweetened condensed milk. Turn speed to low and mix in half of the lime juice. Once the juice is incorporated add the other half of the juice and the zest, continue to mix until blended, just a few seconds. Pour the mixture into the pie shell and bake at 350 degrees for 12 minutes to set the yolks and kill any salmonella in the eggs. If you are using the whipping cream for garish, prepare the cream. Serve with a dollop of whipped cream.

LEMON ANGEL TORTE

4	egg whites
¼	teaspoon cream of tartar
¼	teaspoon salt
1	cup sugar

Beat whites, cream of tartar and salt until soft peaks form. Gradually add sugar and beat until stiff peaks form. Spread in a well buttered 9 inch pie plate - spread on bottom and sides. Bake at 275 degrees for 50 minutes or until browned.

FILLING

4	egg yolks
½	cup sugar
3	tablespoons lemon juice
1	tablespoon grated lemon rind
1	pinch salt

In top of double boiler, heat yolks until thick and lemon colored. Gradually beat in lemon rind, juice, sugar and salt. Cook and stir over boiling water until thick. Cool completely. Whip 1 carton whipping cream and spread half the cream in pie shell. Spoon in the lemon filling and spread remaining whipped cream covering entire shell. Chill several hours or overnight.

LEMON CHESS PIE

2   cups sugar
1   tablespoon all purpose flour
1   tablespoon corn meal
1   pinch salt
¼   cup margarine, melted
¼   cup milk
2   lemons, juice and grated rind
4   eggs, beaten
1   unbaked deep dish pie shell

Combine sugar, flour, corn meal, and salt, mix well. Add butter and milk, mixing well. Add lemon juice, lemon rind and eggs, beat well. Pour into an unbaked pie shell and bake at 350 degrees for 30-35 minutes or until set.

LEMON CREAM PIE

1 cup sugar

⅓ cup cornstarch

¼ teaspoon salt

2 cups scalded very hot milk

2 tablespoons butter

3 egg yolks, beaten

⅓ cup fresh lemon juice

1 teaspoon grated lemon peel

1 egg white

Mix sugar, cornstarch and salt in top of double boiler. Add hot milk slowly, stirring constantly. Add butter, and blend. Cook over boiling water until thick, stirring constantly. Remove from heat and stir a small amount of hot mixture into beaten egg yolks. Add yolks to remaining hot mixture, stirring vigorously. Blend in lemon juice and lemon peel. Return to heat and cook 2 minutes. Remove from heat and fold in stiffly beaten egg white. Cool slightly and pour into baked deep dish pie shell. This can be cooked in the microwave. Stir often.

MERINGUE

3 egg whites

¼ teaspoon cream of tartar

6 tablespoons sugar

¼ teaspoon lemon extract

Beat egg whites on high, cream of tartar and lemon extract until soft peaks form, add sugar 1 tablespoon at a time, beat until stiff peaks form. Spoon over pie and bake at 350 degrees until lightly browned.

LEMON MERINGUE PIE

1   cup sugar
5   tablespoons cornstarch
2   cups water
½   cup lemon juice
1   tablespoon grated lemon rind
3   eggs, separated

Mix sugar and cornstarch, add water, lemon juice and rind. Add beaten egg yolks and cook, stirring constantly until thickened. Pour into baked deep dish pie shell. Top with meringue. Note: This can be cooked in the microwave: stir often.

MERINGUE

3   egg whites
¼   teaspoon cream of tartar
6   tablespoons sugar

Beat whites and cream of tartar on high until soft peaks form. Add 1 tablespoon sugar at a time: continue beating until stiff peaks form. Spoon over pie and bake at 350 degrees until lightly browned.

MACAROON PIE

3   eggs whites
¾   cup sugar
¼   teaspoon baking powder
1   teaspoon almond flavoring
12 saltine crackers, crushed fine
12 chopped dates
1   cup chopped nuts

> Beat egg whites on high until peaks form, add sugar gradually, beating until stiff. Add baking powder and flavoring. Fold in saltines which have been mixed with dates and nuts. Bake in a greased 9 or 10 inch pie plate 30 - 35 minutes. Serve with whipped cream.

MYSTERY PECAN PIE

1   deep dish pie crust
1   8 ounce package cream cheese, softened
4   large eggs, divided
¾   cup sugar, divided
1   cup chopped pecans
1   cup light corn syrup
¼   teaspoon salt
2   teaspoons vanilla, divided

> Beat cream cheese, 1 egg, ½ cup sugar, 1 teaspoon vanilla, and salt at medium speed until smooth. Pour into pie crust. Sprinkle with pecans. Stir together corn syrup, remaining eggs, remaining ¼ cup sugar, and remaining 1 teaspoon vanilla, pour mixture over pecans. Bake at 350 degrees for 50 - 55 minutes or until set.

OLD FASHIONED EGG PIE

1½ cups sugar
3   eggs
½   cup melted butter
¼   cup buttermilk
1   tablespoon flour

> Mix all ingredients together and pour into unbaked deep dish pie shell. Bake at 350 degrees for 1 hour or until knife inserted in center comes out clean.

PEACH PIE

6-8 peaches, sliced
white sandwich bread, de-crusted
1   egg, beaten
1¼   cups sugar
2   tablespoons flour
1   stick butter, melted

> Slice peaches and place in bottom of a buttered 9 x 9 inch baking dish. Cut crust from bread and cut each slice into 3 strips: place on top of peaches, completely covering peaches. Melt butter and mix with sugar and flour. Add egg and mix well. Drizzle over bread. Sprinkle with cinnamon or nutmeg if desired. Bake at 350 degrees for 30 - 35 minutes or until brown.

PEACHES AND CREAM PIE

3   cups fresh chopped peaches
1   9 inch deep dish pie shell, unbaked
1   cup sugar
⅓   cup all purpose flour
⅛   teaspoon salt
2   eggs, beaten
½   cup sour cream

> Place 3 cups peaches in bottom of pie shell. Combine sugar, flour and salt. Add eggs and sour cream stirring until well blended. Spoon over peaches.

TOPPING

½   cup sugar
½   cup all purpose flour
⅛   teaspoon salt
¼   cup butter
1   fresh peach sliced for garnish

> Combine sugar and flour, cut in butter until mixture resembles coarse meal. Sprinkle evenly over pie. Bake at 350 degrees until golden brown. Approximately 30 - 40 minutes. Garnish with sliced peach.

PEANUT BUTTER PIE

½   cup extra crunchy peanut butter
1   8 ounce package cream cheese
¾   cup powdered sugar
1   8 ounce carton Cool Whip
1   Graham cracker pie crust

Mix peanut butter, cream cheese and powdered sugar together. Fold in Cool Whip. Pour into a Graham cracker pie crust.

PECAN PIE

4   eggs, slightly beaten
1   cup sugar
1   cup white Karo syrup
1   teaspoon vanilla
1   cup chopped pecans
2   tablespoons butter
1   unbaked deep dish pie shell

Combine beaten eggs, sugar, Karo syrup, vanilla, pecans and butter. Mix well. Pour into unbaked pie shell. Bake at 325 degrees for 50 minutes or until a silver knife inserted in center comes out clean.

PERFECT CUSTARD PIE

4   eggs, slightly beaten
½   cup sugar
¼   teaspoon salt
1   teaspoon vanilla
½   teaspoon almond extract
2   cups milk, scalded
1   deep dish pie shell
ground nutmeg

Combine eggs, sugar, salt and flavoring: beat until well blended. Gradually stir in scalded milk. Pour into pie shell. Bake at 400 degrees for 15 minutes. Reduce oven temperature to 350 degrees and bake 15 - 20 minutes or until knife inserted in center comes out clean.

PINEAPPLE PIE

⅓   cup sugar

1   tablespoons cornstarch

1   can crushed pineapple

1   8 ounce package cream cheese

½   cup sugar

½   teaspoon salt

2   eggs

½   cup milk

½   teaspoon vanilla extract

¼   cup chopped pecans

1   deep dish unbaked pie shell

Blend ⅓ cup sugar, cornstarch and pineapple. Cook until thick and clear. Cool. Blend cream cheese with ½ cup sugar and salt. Add eggs one at a time. Blend in milk and vanilla. Spread pineapple mixture in unbaked shell. Pour cream cheese mixture on top. Sprinkle pecans on top of this. Bake in 400 degree oven for 50 minutes. Chill and serve.

PUMPKIN PIE

1	15 ounce can pumpkin pie filling	2	eggs beaten
½	teaspoon ginger	1	14 ounce can Eagle Brand condensed milk
¼	teaspoon nutmeg	¼	teaspoon cloves
¾	teaspoon cinnamon		deep dish pie shell

Mix all ingredients together, pour into pie shell and bake at 400 degrees for 50 minutes.

TOPPING

1	cup brown sugar	½	cup flour
1	cup chopped nuts	⅓	stick melted butter

Mix thoroughly and sprinkle on top of pie the last 20 - 25 minutes of baking time. Serve with whip cream.

SCUPPERNONG COBBLER

1	stick butter	1	cup sugar
1	egg	2	cups plain flour
4	teaspoons baking powder	½	teaspoon salt
1	cup milk	1	teaspoon vanilla
2	cups scuppernong hulls	1	cup sugar
2	cups water		

Cream butter and sugar. Add egg and beat well at medium speed. Add dry mixture alternately with milk. Pour in greased baking dish. Boil scuppernong hulls, remove pulp, in 2 cups water for 10 minutes. Stir in the 1 cup sugar. Pour over cake mixture. Do not stir. Bake at 375 degrees for 35 minutes or until browned.

SOUR CREAM LEMON PIE

3	large egg yolks	1	cup sugar
2	tablespoons all purpose flour	¼	cup butter, melted
¼	cup lemon juice	1	tablespoons finely grated
1	cup milk		lemon rind
1	cup sour cream	1	baked deep dish pie crust

Meringue

Beat egg yolks slightly with a wire whisk in top of a double boiler. Add sugar, flour, melted butter, lemon juice, and rind: mix well. Blend in milk and cook about 15 minutes over rapidly boiling water, stirring constantly until mixture thickens. Allow filling to cool then fold in sour cream and pour into pie crust. Note: This filling may be cooked in microwave, stir every 2 minutes until it thickens.

MERINGUE

3   large egg whites
¼   teaspoon cream of tartar
1   tablespoon water
6   tablespoons sugar
⅛   teaspoon salt
1   teaspoon vanilla extract

Beat egg whites, cream of tartar and water in a small bowl on high speed of electric mixer for 3 minutes or until whites begin to stand in peaks. Add sugar, 1 tablespoon at a time. Add salt and vanilla. Continue beating at high speed until whites are stiff. Spread on filled pie crust: be sure meringue completely covers the filling. Bake at 300 degrees for 15 - 20 minutes or until golden brown. If you serve this pie warm, the filling will be slightly runny. When cold, it cuts well.

SWEET POTATO PECAN PIE

1	cup sweet potatoes, mashed	1	cup nuts
½	cup butter	3	eggs
1	cup light corn syrup	1	cup sugar
1	teaspoon vanilla extract	½	teaspoon lemon juice
1	dash salt		unbaked deep dish pie shell

Mix all ingredients together. Pour into pie crust. Bake at 400 degrees for 10 minutes. Reduce heat to 325 degrees and bake for 40 minutes or until set.

SWEET POTATO PIE

2½	cups mashed sweet potatoes	1¼	cups sugar
1	cup milk	¼	cup pineapple juice
¼	cup butter, melted	1	teaspoon vanilla extract
¼	teaspoon salt	¼	teaspoon ground nutmeg
3	large eggs, beaten		

Bake sweet potatoes at 350 degrees until tender. Cool. Peel potatoes and beat until smooth. Add sugar and next 7 ingredients, beating until blended. Pour into unbaked **deep dish** pie crust. Bake at 425 degrees for 15 minutes. Reduce oven temperature to 350 degrees, and bake 1 hour and 20 minutes or until a knife inserted in center comes out clean.

THREE STORY CUSTARD PIE

4   eggs
½   cup sugar
3   cups scalded milk, very hot
½   teaspoon vanilla
1   package dried peaches
sugar to taste
1   unbaked deep dish pie shell

> The day before making pie, cook 1 package of dried peaches until tender. When done, add sugar to taste. Put fruit in refrigerator over night. Spread cooked fruit on bottom of pie shell. Make egg custard by combining eggs and sugar - then slowly add milk and vanilla. Pour on top of fruit and bake at 450 degrees for 10 minutes. Reduce heat to 325 degrees and cook until custard is set. When done, remove from oven and cover with meringue made from 2 of the egg whites. Return to oven and lightly brown.

WHITE CHOCOLATE CHEESE CAKE

1   8 ounce package cream cheese
2   packages Jello white chocolate flavor instant pudding mix
2   cups cold milk, divided
1   8 ounce carton Cool Whip
1   Graham cracker pie crust

> Beat cream cheese and ½ cup milk in large bowl. Add remaining 1 ½ cups milk and pudding mixes. Beat 1 minute. Stir in Cool Whip until well blended. Spoon into crust. Refrigerate until set. Garnish with white chocolate curls made with bakers chocolate.

ICE CREAMS

BUTTER PECAN ICE CREAM

¼   cup butter

2   cups chopped pecans

7   cups milk, divided

1   14 ounce can sweetened condensed milk

2   cups sugar

6   large eggs, lightly beaten

1   5 ounce package vanilla instant pudding mix

1   teaspoon vanilla extract

Melt butter in large saucepan over medium high heat. Add pecans and cook stirring constantly, 3 minutes or until lightly browned. Drain and set aside. Combine 1 cup milk and next 3 ingredients in saucepan, cook over medium heat, stirring constantly, 5 minutes or until mixture coats back of spoon. Cool. Stir in remaining 6 cups milk, pudding mix and vanilla: add pecans, stirring well. Pour into ice cream churn freezer container, 5 quart size. Freeze according to manufacture's directions. Pack freezer with additional ice and rock salt. Let stand 1 hour before serving.

HOME MADE PEACH ICE CREAM

2   pints frozen sweetened   2   cups sugar
    peaches   Ice cream salt
2   large cans evaporated milk   Ice cream freezer
1   quart skim or whole milk   20   pounds crushed ice
1   can condensed milk

Thaw peaches. Blend in blender. Mix sugar, condensed milk and evaporated milk together. Add blended peaches to mixture, pour into ice cream freezer. Add enough milk to fill freezer and churn. Add ice and salt alternately. Keep adding ice and ice cream will freeze faster. Usual time 20 - 30 minutes.

VANILLA ICE CREAM

4   eggs   2   quarts milk
1½ cups sugar   ⅛   teaspoon salt
1   large can evaporated milk

Separate and beat egg yolks and whites of eggs separately. Add sugar and canned evaporated milk to the yolks. Fold in egg whites to which salt has been added. Pour into ice cream churn and fill to line with milk. Freeze and serve.

VANILLA ICE CREAM - FAVORITE

4   eggs   2   cans condensed milk
1   cup sugar   ⅛   teaspoon salt
2   tablespoons vanilla   1½ quarts milk
½   pints whipping cream

Combine eggs, cream, sugar, salt, and vanilla in bowl, mix well. Pour into ice cream churn, add condensed milk and stir well. Add milk to fill line on can and stir. Churn in freezer. Makes 4 quarts. If adding fruit to this ice cream, sweeten the fruit first.

CAKES & FROSTINGS

CAKE BAKING TIPS

1. Sift flour before measuring. Then sift 3 times after measuring.

2. Use accurate measurements, do not guess.

3. For a light textured cake; cream butter or shortening and sugar until light and fluffy. Beat eggs well after each addition. Blend flour in thoroughly but don't over beat after adding flour.

4. If the recipe calls for a liquid, always alternate liquid and flour beginning and ending with the same one.

5. Don't have oven too hot.

6. Wrap outside of tube pan with aluminum foil to prevent cake from getting too brown while baking.

7. Check the expiration date on your baking powder. If it is out of date discard it.

AMBROSIA CAKE

1 cup butter, softened
2 cups sugar
4 eggs
1 teaspoon butter flavoring
1 teaspoon vanilla extract
3 cups sifted cake flour
2½ teaspoons baking powder
½ teaspoon salt
1 cup milk
Orange Filling, page 217
Divinity Frosting, page 217
½ cup flaked coconut

Cream butter and sugar until fluffy, add eggs, one at a time, beating well after each. Add flavorings and beat 2 minutes on high speed with electric mixer. Sift together flour, baking powder and salt, add to creamed mixture alternately with milk, beating on low speed just until blended. Beat on high speed for 1 minute. Pour batter in 3 greased and floured 9 inch cake pans. Bake at 350 degrees for 20 - 25 minutes or until cake tests done. Cool in pans 10 minutes. Remove from pans and cool completely. Spread Orange Filling between layers. Spread top and sides of cake with Divinity Frosting. Sprinkle with coconut.

ORANGE FILLING

1   cup sugar

3   tablespoons cornstarch

¼   teaspoon salt

¾   cup orange juice

¼   cup lemon juice

½   cup water

3   egg yolks, beaten

1   tablespoon grated orange rind

Combine sugar, cornstarch and salt in a small saucepan: gradually stir in fruit juices and water. Cook over medium heat, stirring constantly until mixture thickens and boils. Slowly stir a small amount of hot mixture into egg yolks: add to remaining hot mixture stirring constantly. Boil 1 minute longer, stirring constantly. Remove from heat and stir in orange rind. Let cool. Spread between layers of cake.

DIVINITY FROSTING

1½   cups sugar

½   teaspoon cream of tartar

½   cup water

3   egg whites

½   teaspoon vanilla extract

Combine sugar, cream of tartar and water in a heavy saucepan. Cook over medium heat stirring constantly until mixture is clear. Cook without stirring until candy thermometer reaches 240 degrees. Beat egg whites on high speed until soft peaks form, continue to beat egg whites while slowly adding syrup mixture. Add vanilla, continue beating until stiff peaks form and frosting is thick enough to spread. Spread on cake, sprinkle with ½ cup coconut.

APPLE - COCONUT CAKE

3   cups plain flour
1   teaspoon baking powder
2½ cups sugar
1½ cups corn cooking oil
6   eggs
1   teaspoon vanilla
2   teaspoons fresh lemon juice
1½ cups flake coconut
1   cup chopped nuts
2   cups cut up apple with peeling

> Sift flour and baking powder together. Beat sugar and oil. Add eggs one at a time, then add flour, vanilla and lemon juice. Spoon in coconut, nuts and apples. Bake at 350 degrees 1 hour and 15 minutes.

LEMON GLAZE

½   box powdered sugar
juice of 2 lemons

> Add juice to sugar until it gets about the thickness of a good cake icing, you may not need all the lemon juice Pour over cake while cake is still hot.

BACARDI RUM CAKE

1   cup chopped pecans or walnuts
1   box yellow cake mix
1   package instant vanilla pudding
4   eggs
½   cup cold water
½   cup Wesson oil
½   cup dark Bacardi rum

Grease and flour 10 inch tube pan. Sprinkle nuts over bottom of pan. Mix cake mix, pudding mix, eggs, water, oil and rum together well. Pour batter over nuts. Bake at 325 degrees for 1 hour. Cool. Invert on serving plate. Prick top with toothpick. Drizzle and smooth glaze evenly over top and sides. Allow cake to absorb glaze. Repeat until all the glaze is absorbed.

GLAZE

¼   pound butter
¼   cup water
1   cup sugar
½   cup Bacardi rum

Melt butter, stir in water and sugar. Boil for 5 minutes, stirring constantly. Remove from heat and stir in rum.

BANANA - DATE CAKE

1½ cups chopped dates
1½ cups water
1½ cups mashed bananas
1¼ cups sugar
½ stick butter
2 eggs, separated
1 teaspoon vanilla
3 cups sifted all purpose flour
2 teaspoons baking powder
1 teaspoon baking soda
½ teaspoon salt
1 cup chopped walnuts

Boil dates in water 5 minutes. Cool. Put in large bowl and beat in bananas, butter, sugar, egg yolks and vanilla. Sift together next 4 ingredients and fold into banana mixture. Beat egg whites until stiff and fold into batter with nuts. Spoon into greased and floured Bundt pan. Bake for 50 minutes or until cake tests done. Cool in pan 10 minutes.

BROILER CAKE

1   cup butter

2   cups sugar

3   cups sifted all purpose flour

4   eggs, separated

2   teaspoons baking powder

1   cup milk

1   teaspoon vanilla

Cream together butter and 1 cup sugar. Add well beaten egg yolks. Sift together flour and baking powder and add alternately with the milk beating well after each addition. Add vanilla. Beat egg whites until stiff but not dry. Add remaining cup of sugar to egg whites and fold into the cake batter. Bake in a 13 x 9 x 2 inch pan at 325 degrees approximately 1 hour.

BROILER TOPPING

1   stick butter

1   cup brown sugar

6   tablespoons Carnation milk

1   cup chopped nuts

Beat together butter, sugar and milk. Add nuts. Pour over cake and place under broiler until brown.

BROWN SUGAR POUND CAKE

1	cup shortening	½	cup butter, softened
1	1 pound box light	5	large eggs
	brown sugar	3	cups all purpose flour
½	teaspoon salt	½	teaspoon baking powder
1	cup evaporated milk	1	teaspoon vanilla extract

Beat shortening, butter and brown sugar at medium speed with an electric mixer 2 minutes or until creamy. Add eggs, one at a time, beating well on medium speed after each addition. Combine flour, salt and baking powder, add alternately with milk, beginning and ending with flour mixture. Stir in flavoring. Pour batter into a greased and floured Bundt pan. Bake at 300 degrees for 1 hour and 15 minutes or until a long wooden toothpick inserted in center comes out clean. Cool in pan on a wire rack 15 minutes: remove from pan and cool completely on a wire rack. Pour warm Brown Sugar Glaze over cake. Let cake stand 30 minutes or until glaze is firm.

BROWN SUGAR GLAZE

½	cup butter	1	cup firmly packed light
¼	cup evaporated milk		brown sugar
3	cups powdered sugar, sifted	1	teaspoon vanilla extract

Melt butter in medium saucepan over medium heat. Whisk in brown sugar and cook one minute. Add milk, powdered sugar and vanilla, whisk until creamy. Remove from heat, and pour immediately over cooled cake.

BROWN SUGAR RUM POUND CAKE

1½ cups butter, softened

1   16 ounce package light brown sugar

1   cup sugar

5   large eggs

¾   cup milk

¼   cup dark rum

2   teaspoons vanilla extract

3   cups all purpose flour

1   teaspoon baking powder

¼   teaspoon salt

1   cup chopped pecans

Beat butter at medium speed of mixer about 2 minutes or until creamy. Gradually add sugar, beating 5 - 7 minutes. Add eggs, one at a time beating just until yellow disappears. Combine milk, rum and vanilla. Combine flour, baking powder, and salt, add to butter mixture alternately with milk mixture. Beat at low speed just until blended after each addition. Fold in pecans. Pour batter into greased and floured Bundt or tube pan. Bake at 325 degrees for 1 hour and 20 minutes or until a wooden toothpick inserted in center comes out clean. Cool in pan on a wire rack for 10-15 minutes. Remove cake from pan and let cool completely on wire rack.

BUTTER PECAN COFFEE CAKE

1   15 ounce can crushed
    pineapple
1   can cherries
½   stick butter

1   box butter pecan coffee
    cake mix
½   stick butter

Grease and flour long pan. Pour in pineapple and juice and smooth over bottom of 9 x 13 inch pan. Squeeze juice from cherries and spread on top of pineapple. Cut ½ stick butter and dot around. Spread cake mix over this. Dot other ½ stick of butter over top. Bake at 325 degrees for 1 hour.

CARAMEL PECAN POUND CAKE

1   cup butter
1   cup sugar
5   eggs
½   teaspoon salt
1   cup milk
1   cup finely chopped pecans

1   1 pound box light
    brown sugar
½   teaspoon baking powder
3   cups all purpose flour
1   tablespoon vanilla

Preheat oven to 350 degrees. In large bowl, cream butter and brown sugar. Gradually add sugar and continue creaming. Add eggs one at a time, beating after each. In medium bowl, combine baking powder, salt and flour. Add flour mixture alternately with milk, beginning and ending with flour. Mix just until well blended. Stir in vanilla and pecans. Pour batter into a greased and floured 10 inch tube pan and bake for 1 hour and 30 minutes. Cool before removing from pan.

CARAMEL CAKE

3   cups sugar
½   pound butter
6   eggs
½   pint sour cream
1   teaspoon vanilla flavoring
¼   teaspoon salt in 1 teaspoon hot water
3   cups cake flour
½   teaspoon baking soda in ½ teaspoon hot water

Cream sugar and butter until fluffy, about 10 minutes. Add eggs one at a time, beating well on medium speed after each addition. Add salt and flavoring. Add alternately sour cream and flour. Scald soda and add. Pour into 3 greased and floured cake pans. Bake at 350 degrees for 30 minutes. Cool and frost.

FROSTING

½   pint whipped cream
2   cups sugar
⅔   cup sugar
6   tablespoons butter
1   teaspoon vanilla extract

Mix cream and sugar, let come to a boil and set off. Brown ⅔ cup sugar in cast iron skillet. Add to first mixture and cook to a soft ball stage. Add butter and vanilla, beat until cool enough to spread. If icing is sticky it hasn't cooked long enough.

CARROT CAKE

3   cups finely grated raw carrots
2   cups sugar
1½ cups Wesson oil
4   eggs
3   cups cake flour
2   teaspoons baking powder
1   teaspoon baking soda
½   teaspoon salt
1½ teaspoons cinnamon
1   cup finely chopped nuts

> Mix carrots, sugar, oil and eggs. Mix separately dry ingredients and combine. Bake at 300 degrees in greased tube pan for 1 ½ hours. Allow to cool. Can be baked in layers if desired.

ICING

1   8 ounce package cream cheese
1   box 10 X powdered sugar
1   stick butter
2   teaspoons vanilla

> Cream cheese, sugar and butter together. Add vanilla and beat on medium speed until spreading consistency.

CHOCOLATE POUND CAKE

½   pound butter
½   cup shortening
3   cups sugar
3   cups cake flour
5   eggs
¼   teaspoon baking powder
½   cup cocoa
1   teaspoon vanilla
1¼ cups milk

Cream butter, sugar and shortening real good. Add eggs one at a time beating well after each. Sift dry ingredients together. Add dry ingredients and milk alternately beating on medium speed constantly. Add vanilla. Pour batter in greased and floured tube pan. Bake 1 hour and 25 minutes at 300 degrees. Cool completely before icing.

ICING

½   cup cocoa
1   box 10 X powdered sugar
½   cup butter
8   tablespoons evaporated milk
1   tablespoon vanilla extract
¼   teaspoon almond extract

Sift sugar and cocoa together. Bring milk and butter to a boil. Cream into sugar mixture until spreading consistency. When adding milk, pour slowly, it might take more or less.

COCA COLA CAKE

2   cups plain flour
2   cups sugar
1   cup butter
3   teaspoons cocoa
1   cup Coca Cola
½   cup buttermilk
¼   teaspoon salt
1   teaspoon baking soda
2   large eggs, beaten
1   teaspoon vanilla
1½ cups miniature marshmallows

Sift flour and sugar into a large bowl. Combine butter, cocoa and Cola in saucepan; bring to a boil. Remove from heat and pour over flour mixture. Add buttermilk, salt, baking soda and eggs; blend well. Stir in vanilla and marshmallows. This will be thin batter and marshmallows will float to top. Pour batter into a 13 x 9 x 2 inch greased and lined pan. Bake at 350 degrees for 30-35 minutes. Ice in pan while hot.

ICING

½   cup butter
3   tablespoons cocoa
6   tablespoons coca cola
1   box 10 X powdered sugar
1   cup chopped nuts
1   teaspoon vanilla

Combine butter, cocoa and Coca Cola in saucepan; bring to a boil. Remove from heat and add sugar, nuts and vanilla. Mix well and spread on hot cake.

COCONUT PINEAPPLE CAKE

1	cup butter	2	cups sugar
4	eggs	3	cups sifted cake flour
1	tablespoon baking powder	¼	teaspoon salt
1	cup milk	1	teaspoon vanilla extract
1	teaspoon almond extract		Pineapple Filling
2	cups coconut, divided		Seven Minute Frosting, page 230

Cream butter, gradually add sugar beating well at medium speed of mixer. Add eggs one at a time, beating well after each addition. Combine flour, baking powder and salt, which have been sifted together 3 times. Add to creamed mixture alternately with milk beginning and ending with flour mixture. Mix after each addition. Stir in flavorings. Pour into 3 greased and floured 9 inch cake pans. Bake at 350 degrees for 25 - 30 minutes. Cool.

PINEAPPLE FILLING

1	cup sugar	3	tablespoons all purpose flour
2	eggs, beaten	1	8 ounce can crushed
2	tablespoons lemon juice		pineapple, un-drained
1	tablespoon butter	1	teaspoon vanilla

Combine sugar and flour in small saucepan. Add remaining ingredients. Cook over medium heat stirring constantly until thickened, about 2 minutes. Cool. Spread 1 layer with half of Pineapple Filling, sprinkle ⅓ coconut over filling. Repeat with next cake layer.

7 MINUTE FROSTING

1½ cups sugar
¼ cup + 1 tablespoon cold water
2 egg whites
1 tablespoon light corn syrup
1 dash salt
1 teaspoon vanilla extract

Combine all ingredients, except vanilla, in top of large double boiler. Beat at low speed of mixer, 30 seconds or until just blended. Place over boiling water: beat constantly on high speed 7 minutes or until stiff peaks form. Remove from heat. Add vanilla. Beat 2 minutes until frosting is thick enough to spread. Spread on top and sides of cake and sprinkle with remaining coconut on top.

CRISCO POUND CAKE

2 cups Crisco
2⅔ cups sugar
8 extra large eggs
3½ cups cake flour
½ cup canned milk
1 tablespoon vanilla butter and nut flavoring
pinch of salt

Cream Crisco and sugar well. Add eggs 2 at a time and beat well. Add flavoring into milk and then add milk and flour alternately and blend well. Bake in a greased and floured tube pan, at 325 degrees for 1 hour and 45 minutes.

DATE-NUT CAKE

6	eggs, separated	2	cups sugar
1	cup light brown sugar	¾	pound butter
4	cups plain flour	1	teaspoon baking powder
1	teaspoon nutmeg	2	pounds chopped dates
4	cups chopped pecans		

Cream butter and sugar, add egg yolks, one at a time, and beat well. Add brown sugar, beat well, add nutmeg, half of the flour and baking powder. Dredge nuts and dates with other half of flour: then add to cake batter. Fold in well beaten egg whites. Bake in tube pan 3 - 3 ½ hours at 250 degrees.

DELICIOUS COCONUT CAKE

1   box Pillsbury all butter cake mix

Mix and bake according to directions on package.

FILLING

1	8 ounce carton sour cream	1¼ cups sugar
2	cans coconut	

Mix together and ice cake while it is steaming hot. Cover and refrigerate for 48 hours before cutting. Keep refrigerated.

ICING IF PREFERRED

¼	cup Crisco	1 box 10 X powdered sugar
	sherry	red food color

Add a little canned milk to moisten and then add enough sherry to make it spreading consistency. Beat until fluffy. Add a drop or two of red food coloring to make slightly pink.

DUMP CAKE

1   15 ounce can crushed pineapple, drained
1   15 ounce can cherry pie filling
1   box white or yellow cake mix
1   cup chopped nuts
1   stick butter, melted

> Grease a tube pan or an oblong baking dish. Add ingredients in order given, just sprinkling the cake mix on top of the pie filling. Add nuts and pour the melted butter over the top. Bake at 350 degrees for 45 minutes - 1 hour. Spoon out to serve. Whipped cream is delicious on top.

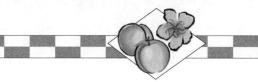

FIG PRESERVE CAKE

1½ cups sugar	2 cups all purpose flour
1 teaspoon baking soda	1 teaspoon salt
1 teaspoon nutmeg	1 teaspoon cinnamon
½ teaspoon allspice	½ teaspoon ground cloves
1 cup vegetable oil	3 eggs
1 cup buttermilk	1 tablespoon vanilla extract
1 cup fig preserves, chopped	½ cup chopped pecans
Buttermilk Glaze	or walnuts

Combine dry ingredients in a large bowl: add oil, beating well. Add eggs and beat well, add buttermilk and vanilla, mixing thoroughly. Stir in preserves and nuts. Pour batter into a greased and floured 10 inch tube pan: bake at 350 degrees for 1 hour and 15 minutes. Let cool 10 minutes then remove from pan. Pour warm Buttermilk Glaze over warm cake.

BUTTERMILK GLAZE

¼ cup buttermilk	½ cup sugar
¼ teaspoon baking soda	1½ teaspoons cornstarch
¼ cup butter	1½ teaspoons vanilla

Combine first 5 ingredients in a saucepan, bring to a boil and remove from heat. Cool slightly and stir in vanilla. Pour over warm cake.

FIVE FLAVOR CAKE

1	cup butter	½	cup shortening
3	cups sugar	5	eggs, well beaten
3	cups all purpose flour	½	teaspoon baking powder
1	cup milk	1	teaspoon coconut extract
1	teaspoon rum extract	1	teaspoon butter extract
1	teaspoon lemon extract	1	teaspoon vanilla extract

Glaze, optional

Cream butter, shortening, and sugar until light and fluffy. Add eggs. Combine flour and baking powder. Add to creamed mixture alternately with milk. Stir in extracts. Spoon mixture into a greased and floured Bundt or tube pan. Bake at 325 degrees for 1 hour and 15 minutes or until cake tests done. Add glaze if desired. Pour ½ of glaze while cake is in pan. Cool in pan for 10 minutes. Remove and pour remaining glaze over cake.

GLAZE

1	cup sugar	½	cup water
1	teaspoon coconut extract	1	teaspoon rum extract
1	teaspoon vanilla extract	1	teaspoon lemon extract
1	teaspoon almond extract		

Combine all ingredients in a saucepan, bring to a boil stirring until sugar is melted.

FRESH APPLE CAKE

1½ cups salad oil

2 cups sugar

3 eggs

3 cups plain flour

1 teaspoon baking soda

½ teaspoon salt

2 teaspoons vanilla

3 cups apples, peeled and chopped fine

1 cup flaked coconut, optional

1 cup chopped nuts

Preheat oven to 325 degrees. Mix oil and sugar: add eggs. Sift together flour, salt and soda. Add to first mixture. Beat until well blended. Stir in apples, nuts and coconut. Place in greased tube pan. Bake for 1 hour or until test done. Have topping ready as cake is removed from oven. Cool cake for 10 minutes. Remove from pan.

TOPPING

1 cup light brown sugar

½ cup butter

½ cup milk

Mix all ingredients in small saucepan. Heat and stir until well blended. Boil 2 minutes. Pour topping over hot cake and allow to soak in. Serve with whipped cream or Cool Whip.

FRESH COCONUT CAKE

1   cup butter
2   cups sugar
4   eggs
3   cups all purpose flour
2   teaspoons baking powder
1   teaspoon salt
1   cup milk
1   teaspoon vanilla

> Cream butter and sugar until light and fluffy. Add eggs, one at a time beating well after each addition. Sift together flour, baking powder and salt, add to creamed mixture alternately with milk, blending well after each addition. Blend in flavoring. Spoon batter into 4 - 5 greased and floured 9 inch cake pans. Bake at 350 degrees for 18 minutes. Cool completely and spread Coconut Filling between layers.

COCONUT FILLING

coconut milk from 1 coconut
3   cups sugar
1   coconut, grated

> Combine coconut milk with enough milk to make 1 ½ cups liquid. If not using fresh coconut: use 1 cup evaporated milk and ½ cup homogenized milk. Combine liquid and sugar in a saucepan. Bring to a boil, cool until slightly thickened, stirring constantly. Remove from heat and add 2 cups grated coconut. Cool and spread on cake.

GERMAN CHOCOLATE CAKE

1	4 ounce package Baker's German Sweet Chocolate	2½	cups sifted Swans Down cake flour
½	cup boiling water	½	teaspoon salt
1	cup butter or margarine	1	teaspoon baking soda
2	cups sugar	1	cup buttermilk
4	egg yolks	4	egg whites, stiffly beaten
1	teaspoon vanilla		

Melt chocolate in boiling water. Cool. Cream butter and sugar until fluffy. Add egg yolks one at a time, and beat well after each. Add melted chocolate and vanilla. Mix well. Sift together flour, salt and baking soda. Add alternately with buttermilk to chocolate mixture, beating after each addition until smooth. Fold in beaten egg whites. Pour into three 8 or 9 inch cake pans, lined on bottom with wax paper. Bake at 350 degrees for 30 - 40 minutes. Cool.

COCONUT - PECAN FROSTING

1	cup evaporated milk	1	cup sugar
3	egg yolks	½	cup butter or margarine
1	teaspoon vanilla	1⅓	cups coconut
½	cup chopped pecans	½	cup chopped walnuts

Combine milk, sugar, beaten egg yolks, butter, and vanilla. Cook and stir over medium heat until thickened - about 12 minutes. Remove from heat: add coconut and nuts. Beat until thick enough to spread. Note: I double this frosting recipe so it will cover the cake completely. It may also be cooked in the microwave until thick, stir often.

ICE BOX FRUIT CAKE

1   16 ounce box vanilla wafers,   1½ cups chopped nuts
    finely crushed   1   pound seedless raisins
1   jar cherries, drained   1   14 ounce can Eagle
                                        Brand milk

Mix nuts, raisins, cherries and vanilla wafers. Add milk gradually, mix thoroughly. Place in lined loaf pan and refrigerate for 24 hours before serving. Keep refrigerated.

ITALIAN CREAM CAKE

2   cups sugar   1   stick butter
1   cup shortening   5   eggs, separated
2   cups sifted plain flour   1   teaspoon baking soda
½   teaspoon salt   2   cups coconut
1   cup chopped pecans   1   tablespoon vanilla
1   cup buttermilk

Cream sugar and shortening together well, add butter and beat on medium until fluffy. Add egg yolks, one at a time, beating well after each. Add the vanilla and buttermilk alternately with the flour and soda, which have been sifted together. Mix well. Add coconut and pecans, fold in beaten egg whites. Pour in 3 greased and floured layer cake pans and bake at 350 degrees for 30 minutes. Cool and frost.

CREAM CHEESE FROSTING

1   8 ounce package   1   stick butter
    cream cheese   1   teaspoon vanilla
1   box 10 X powdered sugar

Soften cream cheese and butter, combine with vanilla and sugar. Beat until creamy. Spread on cake.

JIFFY COCONUT CAKE

CAKE

1   package yellow cake mix

Bake according to directions on package in sheet cake pan.

TOPPING

1   15 ounce can Lopez cream of coconut
1   can Eagle Brand milk

Mix together and pour over cake, while cake is hot.

COCONUT TOPPING

1   12 ounce carton Cool Whip
1   7 ounce can coconut, save ½ cup

Mix together. Spoon over glaze. Sprinkle with remaining ½ cup coconut.

KEY LIME POUND CAKE

CAKE

1   cup butter

½   cup Crisco

2   cups white granulated sugar

5   eggs

3   cups all purpose flour

½   teaspoon baking powder

½   cup milk

½   cup key lime juice

1½   teaspoons vanilla

Preheat oven to 325 degrees. Grease and flour 10 inch tube pan. Mix together the flour and baking powder. Cream together butter, shortening and sugar until light and fluffy. Beat in the eggs one at a time. Beat in the flour mixture alternately with the milk, mixing just until incorporated. Stir in key lime juice and vanilla extract. Pour batter into prepared pan. Bake in pre-heated oven for 90 minutes or until a toothpick inserted into the center of the cake comes out clean. Allow to cool in pan 10 minutes. Turn it out onto a wire rack. While warm, prick top of cake with toothpick. Pour Key Lime Glaze over warm cake. Cool completely.

KEY LIME GLAZE

¼   cup white sugar

¼   cup butter

3   tablespoons Key Lime juice

In small saucepan, combine sugar, butter and Key Lime juice. Bring to a boil. Continue to boil, stirring constantly for 1 minute. Remove from heat. Pour over warm cake.

LEMON PIE CAKE

1   box Lemon Supreme cake mix

Cook cake layers according to directions on package. If recipe calls for 1 cup water, add ½ cup water and ½ cup milk.

GLAZE

2-3 ounces lemon juice fresh, squeezed is better
10 X powdered sugar

Mix together lemon juice and powdered sugar until a soupy glaze has been created. Pour this over hot cake layers when they come out of the oven. Let layers cool completely.

ICING

1   can condensed milk
1   12 ounce carton Cool Whip
6   ounces lemon juice fresh squeezed

Mix Cool Whip and milk, then add lemon juice a little at a time. Frost cake layers.

LEMON SUPREME CAKE

1	box Lemon Supreme Deluxe Cake mix	½	cup sugar
		4	eggs
1	cup apricot nectar	¾	cup Crisco oil

Blend all ingredients in large bowl. Beat at medium speed for 2 minutes. Bake in 3 layers for 45 minutes. Cool.

FROSTING

¼	cup butter	¼	cup cream cheese
4	tablespoons lemon juice	1½	boxes 10 X powdered sugar
1	cup finely chopped nuts		

Add enough evaporated milk to make a good spreading consistency. Mix well and spread on cool cake.

MAPLE NUT CAKE

½	cup Crisco shortening	2	sticks butter
2	cups sugar	1	cup light brown sugar
5	eggs	3	cups cake flour
½	teaspoon baking powder	1	cup milk
1	teaspoon maple extract		
1	cup finely chopped pecans or walnuts		

Cream together Crisco, butter, and sugars. Add eggs one at a time beating well on medium speed after each. Sift flour and baking powder together and add alternately with milk. Add maple extract and nuts. Pour into a greased and floured tube pan, bake at 325 degrees for 1 hour and 15 minutes.

MILLION DOLLAR POUND CAKE

3   cups sugar
1   pound butter, softened
6   eggs, at room temperature
4   cups all purpose flour
¾   cup milk
1   teaspoon almond extract
1   teaspoon vanilla extract

Combine sugar and butter, cream until light and fluffy. Add eggs, one at a time, beating well on medium after each addition. Add flour to creamed mixture alternately with milk, blend well. Add flavorings. Pour batter into a well greased and floured 10 inch tube pan. Bake at 300 degrees for 1 hour and 40 minutes or until cake tests done.

ORANGE SLICE CANDY CAKE

1   cup butter, softened

2   cups sugar

4   eggs

3   cups cake flour

½   cup buttermilk

1   teaspoon baking soda

1   teaspoon salt

1   teaspoon vanilla

1   teaspoon lemon extract

1   pound orange slice candy

1   8 ounce box dates 27 slices

2   cups chopped nuts

1½ cups flake coconut

½   cup cake flour

> Dredge the candy, dates, nuts and coconut in the ½ cup flour.
> Cream butter and sugar. Add eggs one at a time beating well on
> medium speed after each. Mix baking soda in milk. Add milk
> and flour alternately. Add fruit mixture. Pour into a greased and
> floured tube pan, bake 2 ½ hours at 250 degrees. Pour glaze
> over cake while hot.

GLAZE

1   cup brown sugar

1   cup orange juice

> Dissolve sugar in juice and pour over hot cake.

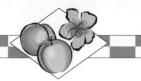

PINEAPPLE POUND CAKE

½ cup Crisco	½ pound butter
2¾ cups sugar	6 large eggs
3 cups sifted all purpose flour	1 teaspoon baking powder
¼ cup milk	1 teaspoon vanilla
¾ cup drained	¼ cup butter
crushed pineapple	1½ cups powdered sugar
1 cup crushed pineapple, drained	

Cream Crisco, butter and sugar. Add eggs, one at a time, beating well on medium after each. Add flour sifted with baking powder, alternately with milk. Add vanilla, stir in crushed pineapple and juice and blend well. Pour batter into greased and floured 10 inch tube pan. Place in cold oven. Turn oven to 325 degrees and bake for 1 ½ hours or until top springs back when lightly touched. Let stand for few minutes in pan. Combine butter, powdered sugar and about 1 cup drained pineapple. Pour over cake, after removing from pan, while cake is still hot.

POPPY SEED CAKE

1   package yellow cake mix

4   eggs

¾   cup oil

1   cup water

½   jar poppy seed

2   packages, small instant butterscotch pudding mix

Mix together well. Bake at 350 degrees for 1 hour.

PRALINE CRUNCH CAKE

1½   cups Graham cracker crumbs
¾   cup brown sugar
¾   cup butter, melted
½   cup chopped pecans
1   package Pillsbury yellow cake mix
¾   cup water
⅓   cup oil
¼   cup Praline Liqueur
3   eggs

> Mix together Graham cracker crumbs, brown sugar, melted butter, and chopped pecans. Pat into a 9 x 13 inch baking dish. Mix together the cake mix, water, oil, liqueur and eggs. Pour over crumb layer. Bake at 375 degrees for 25 - 35 minutes. Cool 10 minutes and turn cake onto sheet cake plate. Cool completely before frosting.

FROSTING

1   cup Pillsbury Vanilla Supreme frosting
1   8 ounce carton Cool Whip
1   teaspoon Praline Liqueur

> Mix together and spread over cake. Cut into squares and serve.

RUBY SLIPPER CAKE

1   package yellow cake mix
with pudding

1   cup sour cream

¼   cup water

2   eggs

1   3 ounce package raspberry
flavored Jello

Combine cake mix, sour cream, water, and eggs in large bowl. Blend, then beat at medium speed 2 minutes until creamy. Spoon ⅓ of batter into well greased and floured 10 inch tube pan. Sprinkle with ½ the Jello. Repeat layers. Spread remaining batter over Jello to cover. Bake at 350 degrees for 45 - 50 minutes or until cake springs back when lightly pressed. Cool in pan for 5 minutes. Remove from pan. Cool on rack. Sprinkle with powdered sugar if desired.

SNOWDRIFT MARDI GRAS CAKE

½   pound butter

1   8 ounce package cream
cheese

1½   cups sugar

1½   teaspoons vanilla

4   large eggs

2¼   cups cake flour

2   teaspoons baking powder

2   cups mixed candied fruit

¼   cup sifted cake flour

½   cup coarsely chopped nuts

½   cup finely chopped nuts

powdered sugar

Thoroughly blend butter, softened cream cheese, sugar and vanilla. Add eggs one at a time beating well after each. Sift together the 2 ¼ cups flour and baking powder. Add to butter mixture and blend well. Dredge fruit and coarse nuts in the remaining ¼ cup flour. Fold into batter. Spoon into greased and floured Bundt pan which has been sprinkled with fine nuts. Bake at 325 degrees for 70 - 80 minutes. Cool in pan for 5 minutes. Turn out and rub with powdered sugar.

SOUR CREAM POUND CAKE

1½ cups butter, room temperature
3 cups sugar
6 large eggs, room temperature
1 cup sour cream

3 cups sifted plain flour
½ teaspoon baking soda
⅛ teaspoon salt
½ teaspoon vanilla extract
½ teaspoon almond extract

Cream butter until the consistency of whipped cream. Add sugar and beat well. Add eggs, one at a time, beating well after each. Stir in sour cream. Sift flour, soda and salt together 3 times: add ½ cup at a time to creamed mixture. Add flavoring. Pour into greased and lined with wax paper tube pan. Bake at 325 degrees for 1 ¼ - 1 ½ hours.

STRAWBERRY CAKE

1 box white cake mix
4 eggs
1 cup Wesson oil
1 5 ounce box fresh or frozen strawberries

1 3 ounce package strawberry Jello dissolved in ½ cup hot water

Beat eggs, add oil and mix well, add cake mix and beat well. Add Jello dissolved in hot water and mix well. Bake in 3 layers at 350 degrees for 30 - 35 minutes.

FILLING

1 box 4 X powdered sugar
½ stick butter

1 5 ounce box fresh or frozen strawberries, without juice

Blend together and spread on cake.

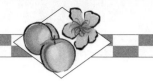

STRAWBERRY CRUNCH CAKE

2	10 ounce packages frozen sliced strawberries, thawed	2	cups all purpose flour
		1	teaspoon baking powder
½	teaspoon baking soda	½	teaspoon salt
1¼	cups sugar	1	cup butter, softened
2	eggs	1	8 ounce cup sour cream
⅓	cup firmly packed light brown sugar	1	cup chopped pecans
		1	teaspoon ground cinnamon
Strawberry Glaze			whipping cream

Drain strawberries, reserving juice for glaze. Combine flour, baking powder, soda, and salt, set aside. Combine 1 ¼ cups sugar and butter, creaming well. Add eggs, beating on medium until smooth. Slowly mix in sour cream. Add flour mixture and stir well. Combine brown sugar, pecans and cinnamon, set aside for topping. Pour half of batter into a greased 13 x 9 x 2 inch baking pan. Spoon strawberries over batter: sprinkle with half of topping mixture. Top with remaining batter and sprinkle with remaining topping. Bake at 350 degrees for 30 - 35 minutes or until cake tests done. Let cool. Cut into squares. Top each square with glaze and whipped cream.

STRAWBERRY GLAZE

reserved strawberry juice
1   tablespoon cornstarch + 1 teaspoon cornstarch
2   teaspoons lemon juice

Combine strawberry juice and cornstarch in a small saucepan, cook over medium heat, stirring constantly, until thickened. Remove from heat: stir in lemon juice. Serve warm over cake. Note: This glaze can be cooked in the microwave in a few short minutes: stir occasionally.

STRAWBERRY REFRIGERATOR CAKE

1   package Duncan Hines Moist Deluxe Strawberry Supreme cake mix
2   10 ounce packages sweetened, frozen sliced strawberries, thawed

Preheat oven to 350 degrees. Grease and flour a 13 x 9 inch baking pan. For cake, prepare, bake and cool following directions on package. Poke holes 1 inch apart in top of cake using handle of wooden spoon. Puree thawed strawberries with juice in blender. Spoon evenly over top of cake allowing mixture to soak into holes.

TOPPING

1   small package vanilla instant pudding and pie filling mix
1   cup milk
2   cups Cool Whip
fresh strawberries, optional

Prepare pudding mix according to directions on package using 1 cup of milk. Fold Cool Whip into pudding mixture. Spread over cake. Garnish with fresh strawberries. Refrigerate at least 4 hours.

TOASTED BUTTER PECAN CAKE

2   cups chopped pecans
1¼ cups butter
3   cups all purpose flour
2   teaspoons baking powder
½   teaspoon salt
2   cups sugar
4   eggs
1   cup milk
2   teaspoons vanilla

Toast pecans in the ¼ cup butter in 350 degrees oven for 20 - 30 minutes, stir frequently. Cream 1 cup butter, add sugar and cream well. Add eggs one at a time beating well on medium speed after each. Add dry ingredients, which have been sifted together, alternately with milk. Stir in vanilla and 1 ⅓ cups pecans. Bake in 3 greased and floured 9 inch cake pans for 25 minutes at 350 degrees. Cool.

BUTTER PECAN FROSTING

¼   cup butter
1   pound sifted 10 X powdered sugar
1   teaspoon vanilla
4-6 tablespoons evaporated milk

Cream all ingredients until spreading consistency. Stir in remaining pecans from the cake recipe. Spread on cake.

TUNNEL OF FUDGE CAKE

1½ cups butter
6 eggs
1½ cups sugar
2 cups cake flour
1 package Pillsbury Double Dutch Fudge Buttercream
Frosting mix, no substitute
2 cups chopped walnuts

> Cream butter in large mixing bowl on high speed of mixer. Add
> eggs, one at a time, beating well after each. At low speed, gradu-
> ally add flour and sugar, mixing until well blended. By hand, stir
> in frosting mix and walnuts, blend well. Pour batter into greased
> Bundt pan or 10 inch tube pan. Bake at 350 degrees for 65 - 70
> minutes. Cool 2 hours. Remove from pan, cool completely before
> serving. Note: The nuts and specific type of frosting mix are es-
> sential to the success of this cake. Test doneness after 65 minutes
> by looking for dry shiny, brownie type crust.

VANILLA WAFER CAKE

6 eggs
½ cup milk
1 12 ounce box vanilla wafers, crushed
1 cup chopped nuts
2 cups coconut
2 sticks butter, softened
1¾ cups sugar

> Cream butter, add sugar and cream well. Add eggs one at a time,
> mixing well. Add Vanilla wafers, blend well, then stir in milk.
> Stir in nuts and coconut. Pour into a greased tube pan. Bake
> at 325 degrees for about 1 hour or until toothpick inserted in
> center comes out clean.

WALDORF ASTORIA
RED CAKE SPECIAL

1   cup Crisco
1½ cups sugar
2   eggs
1   2 ounce red food coloring
2½ cups cake flour
2   tablespoons cocoa
1   teaspoon salt
1   cup buttermilk
1   teaspoon vanilla
1   tablespoon vinegar
1   teaspoon baking soda

Cream Crisco and sugar well. Add eggs one at a time and beat well on medium speed. Sift dry ingredients together 3 times, add to mixture alternately with buttermilk. Add vanilla, vinegar, and baking soda and stir into mixture. Grease and flour 2, 9 inch cake pans. Bake at 350 degrees for 40 minutes.

FILLING

1   cup milk
¼   cup flour
1   cup sugar
1   cup butter
1   teaspoon vanilla

Cook milk and flour together in top of a double boiler, stirring constantly until thick and creamy. Cool. Cream sugar and butter well. Add flour mixture to sugar mixture and add vanilla. Spread on cake when cake is cold. Note: The flour and milk can be cooked in the microwave until thick and creamy, stir often.

WHIPPED CREAM CAKE

2   cups self rising flour
2   cups sugar
2   cups whipping cream, not whipped
4   eggs

> Mix all ingredients well. Pour into 2 floured and greased loaf pans or one 13-inch pan. Bake 25 - 30 minutes at 350 degrees: be sure not to over cook.

WHITE CHOCOLATE POUND CAKE

1   cup Crisco
3   cups sifted cake flour
2½   cups sugar
¼   cup hot water
¼   pound white chocolate
¾   cup milk
6   eggs
1   teaspoon vanilla

> Mix shortening and sugar, beat well on medium speed. Add eggs, one at a time, beating well after each. Mix together water and white chocolate in top of double boiler until chocolate melts: cool, then add to sugar mixture. Add flour and milk alternately, beginning and ending with flour. Add vanilla. Bake at 300 degrees for 1 hour and 15 minutes in a large tube pan.

COOKIES
and
CANDIES

Index

49' ERS

2   cups Bisquick mix
1   box light brown sugar
4   eggs
1½ cups nuts
powdered sugar, if desired

Mix all ingredients together and bake at 325 degrees for 45 minutes. Do not over cook. Cool and cut into squares. Dust with powdered sugar if desired.

ALMOND BARK CRUNCH

5   cups Corn Chex
5   cups Cheerios
1   pound salted nuts
1   pound bag small pretzels
1   pound almond bark

Melt almond bark and mix in other ingredients. Drop on wax paper to dry and break apart.

AMAZING COOKIE

1	box yellow cake mix	2	eggs, beaten
½	cup cooking oil	2	tablespoons water
1	6 ounce bag chocolate chips		

Mix all ingredients until well blended. Add 1 cup chopped nuts and one 6 ounce bag chocolate chips. Drop by teaspoonfuls on greased cookie sheet. Bake at 350 degrees 10 - 12 minutes until lightly browned. VARIATIONS: Nuts and coconut, nuts and butterscotch morsels, nuts and peanut butter morsels, or nuts alone. Remarkably delicious and easy!

ANGEL BROWNIES

1	cup butter	2	cups sugar
1½	cups all purpose flour	2	cups chopped nuts
¼	teaspoon salt	4	eggs
4	squares semi sweet chocolate		

Melt butter and chocolate over hot water. Cream eggs and sugar, then add salt, flour and nuts. Bake in large pan lined with wax paper in 300 degree oven for 25 minutes. Cool and turn out on a cookie sheet and remove paper. Turn cake back into pan. Add a package of large marshmallows on top of cake placing them about 1 inch apart. Return to oven: when marshmallows puff: remove from oven and flatten with a fork until they touch. Cool and frost.

FROSTING

½	cup cocoa	1	box 10 X powdered sugar
½	cup butter	8	tablespoons evaporated milk
1	tablespoon vanilla	¼	teaspoon almond extract

Sift sugar and cocoa together. Bring milk and butter to boil in heavy saucepan. Cream into sugar mixture until you reach a spreading consistency. When adding milk, pour slowly because it might take more or less.

APRICOT BALLS

3   6 ounce packages dried apricots, cut into small pieces
1   14 ounce package flaked coconut
1   cup chopped nuts
1   14 ounce can Eagle Brand condensed milk
½   cup powdered sugar

> Combine apricots, coconut and nuts in a large mixing bowl: add condensed milk, mixing well. Shape in 1 inch balls, and roll each in powdered sugar.

BLONDIES

1   7 ounce jar macadamia nuts, chopped
1¼   cups all purpose flour
½   cup sugar
½   cup packed light brown sugar
¾   stick butter, softened
1¼   teaspoons baking powder
½   teaspoon salt
1½   teaspoons vanilla extract

> Preheat oven to 350. Grease a 9 x 9 inch baking pan. Reserve ½ cup chopped macadamia nuts. Into large bowl, measure flour, remaining ingredients and remaining macadamia nuts. With mixer at low speed, beat until well blended. Spread mixture in pan. Sprinkle reserved macadamia nuts on top. Bake 35 minutes or until toothpick inserted in center comes out clean. Cool and cut into squares.

BRANDY BALLS

1   12 ounce package crushed vanilla wafers
½   cup rum
½   cup brandy
½   cup honey
1   pound ground walnuts
powdered sugar

Mix first 5 ingredients together well. Roll into small balls. Gently roll in powdered sugar and store in tightly covered container in refrigerator. These will keep for 5 weeks. Yields: about 50 balls.

BUCKEYES

1½ boxes 10 X powdered sugar
1   12 ounce jar creamy peanut butter
2   sticks butter
1   cup chopped nuts
1   6 ounce package chocolate morsels
½   block paraffin

Mix sugar, peanut butter, butter and chopped nuts together. Roll in 1 inch balls and refrigerate. Melt chocolate morsels with paraffin over boiling water. Put a toothpick in chilled peanut butter balls and dip ¾ of the way in chocolate mixture. Place on wax paper.

BUTTERSCOTCH BARS

1½ sticks butter
1   cup light brown sugar
1   cup white sugar, granulated
2   eggs, beaten
2   cups all purpose flour
1½ teaspoons salt
1   pinch baking soda
1   teaspoon vanilla
1   cup coarsely chopped nuts
¾   teaspoon baking powder

Mix all ingredients together until well blended. Spoon onto a 9 x 9 inch well greased and floured pan. Bake at 325 degrees for 45 - 50 minutes. Do not overcook. Cut into bars while warm, remove from pan when cool. Chocolate chip morsels or butterscotch morsels may be added if desired.

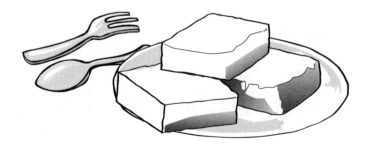

CARAMEL PUFFED CORN

1   6 ounce bag butter flavored puffed corn
1   cup brown sugar
½   cup light Karo syrup
1   teaspoon baking soda
½   stick butter
1   cup chopped pecans

Bring to a boil the brown sugar, Karo syrup and butter. Stir for 2 minutes. Remove from heat. Add baking soda. Mixture will foam. In a large bowl mix puffed corn and nuts. Pour brown sugar mixture over puffed corn and nuts. Stir until all puffed corn is coated. Line jelly roll pan with foil. Pour mixture in pan. Bake at 325 for 25 minutes.

CHEESE NUT ICE BOX WAFERS

2   cups plain flour
1   stick butter
½   teaspoon salt
2   cups grated cheese
dash red pepper
1   cup chopped nuts

Mix all ingredients together well. Add 1 cup chopped nuts. Chill 24 hours. Shape in 2 rolls. Slice real thin. Bake on greased cookie sheet at 350 degrees for 10 - 12 minutes.

CHESS BARS

1   butter recipe cake mix
4   eggs
1   stick butter
1   8 ounce cream cheese, softened
1   teaspoon vanilla
1   1 pound box 10 X powdered sugar
1   cup chopped nuts

Mix cake mix, 1 egg, butter and nuts well. Press into greased 9 x 13 inch pan. Soften cream cheese and beat with 3 eggs. Add vanilla and beat. Blend in powdered sugar and beat until smooth. Pour over pressed mixture and bake 1 hour at 300 degrees.

CHEWY PECAN DELIGHTS

½   cup Crisco
½   cup butter
2½ cups brown sugar
2   eggs, well beaten
2½ cups plain flour
¼   teaspoon salt
½   teaspoon baking soda
1   cup chopped nuts

Cream Crisco and sugar: add eggs and beat well. Add dry ingredients which have been sifted together. Blend together well, stir in nuts. Drop by teaspoonfuls on greased cookie sheets. Bake at 350 degrees for 10-12 minutes.

CHOCOLATE COVERED CHERRIES

2   boxes 4 X powdered sugar
1   quart chopped nuts
1   14 ounce can Eagle Brand milk
4   tablespoons butter
1   tablespoon vanilla
1½   packages chocolate chips
¾   paraffin, block
50   cherries

Mix butter, milk, vanilla, and sugar. You can use some of the cherry juice instead of milk. Candy must be stiff. Add nuts to mixture. Make into balls with a cherry in the center. Refrigerate 3 to 4 hours until firm. Melt chocolate and paraffin in top of double boiler. Dip balls in chocolate mixture with toothpicks and place on wax paper.

CHOW MEIN CLUSTERS

2   6 ounce packages butterscotch morsels
1   6 ¾ ounce can cashew nuts or mixed nuts
1   5 ounce can chow mein noodles

Melt butterscotch morsels in double boiler: add nuts and noodles. Stir lightly until well blended. Drop by spoonfuls onto waxed paper. For variations: stir ½ - 1 cup peanut butter into butterscotch mixture and add 2 cups miniature marshmallows with the nuts and noodles.

CHRISTMAS COOKIES

6   slices candied pineapple

2   cups candied cherries

3   cups chopped dates

½   box white seedless raisins

7   cups chopped nuts

1   cup light brown sugar

1   cup butter

4   eggs

1   teaspoon cinnamon

1   teaspoon soda

½   cup buttermilk

3   cups cake flour, sifted before measuring

½   cup flour to dredge fruit

1   teaspoon vanilla

Use extra flour to dredge fruit and nuts. Cream butter and sugar. Add eggs. Add dry ingredients which have been sifted together, alternating with milk. Drop from teaspoon on greased cookie sheet. Bake at 325 degrees for 10 - 15 minutes until lightly browned.

CHRISTMAS COOKIES - FAVORITE

2   16 ounce packages red candied cherries, chopped
1   16 ounce package green candied cherries, chopped
3   cups cake flour, sifted before measuring
7   cups chopped nuts
1   cup light brown sugar
1   cup butter
4   eggs, beaten
1   teaspoon soda
½   cup flour to dredge fruit
1   teaspoon vanilla
½   cup buttermilk

Use extra flour to dredge fruit and nuts. Cream butter and sugar, add eggs. Add dry ingredients which have been sifted together with milk. Mix candied fruits and nuts into batter. Drop from teaspoon onto greased cookie sheet. Bake at 325 for 10 - 15 minutes until lightly brown.

COCONUT DELIGHTS

1   cup butter   ½   cup sugar
2   cups all purpose flour   1   teaspoon vanilla
1   cup coconut   powdered sugar

Cream butter, add sugar gradually and cream together well. Sift flour and add to creamed mixture gradually. Add vanilla and coconut. Chill 3 to 4 hours. Roll into 1 inch balls. Place on greased cookie sheet and flatten with fork dipped in cold water. Bake at 350 degrees for 15 - 20 minutes. Cool and toss in powdered sugar.

CORNFLAKE CRUNCHIES

2   cups sugar
1   cup light Karo syrup
2   cups crunchy peanut butter
6   cups corn flakes

> Bring sugar and syrup to a boil. Turn heat off and add peanut butter. Mix until creamy. Add corn flakes, 2 cups at a time. Stir and coat well. Place by teaspoonful on wax paper and chill.

CRESCENTS

1¾ sticks butter
2   cups all purpose flour sifted 6 times
6   tablespoons powdered sugar
1   teaspoon vanilla
1½ cups chopped nuts

> Cream butter, add other ingredients and mix thoroughly. Shape with fingers in crescents ½ inch thick and about 3 inches long. Arrange on buttered cookie sheet. Bake at 300 degrees for 20 - 25 minutes. Cool. Roll in powdered sugar. Yields: 36.

CRISPY TEA CAKES

1   cup butter
⅔   cup sugar
1   egg
2½ cups self rising flour
½   teaspoon baking powder
1   teaspoon vanilla
⅛   teaspoon salt

Cream butter and sugar. Add eggs and mix well. Add all dry
ingredients which have been sifted together. Add vanilla. Roll
out on floured board and cut with cookie cutter. Bake at 400
degrees for approximately 10 minutes.

CROCK POT CANDY

2   1 pound packages almond bark, vanilla
1   12 ounce package chocolate chips
1   4 ounce package German chocolate
1   24 ounce can dry roasted peanuts

Put all ingredients in crock pot and cook 2 hours on high. Stir
after cooking. Drop on wax paper with tablespoon. Cool and
serve.

DATE BARS

3   eggs
1   cup powdered sugar
1   teaspoon vanilla
1   tablespoon melted shortening
¼   cup flour
¼   teaspoon salt
½   teaspoon baking powder
¾   cup chopped nuts
1   cup chopped dates

Beat on medium speed eggs, add sugar, melted shortening and vanilla and beat well. Add nuts and dates. Bake at 325 for 25 minutes.

DATE NUT BALLS OR LOGS

½   cup butter
1   8 ounce package chopped dates
1   cup sugar
1   egg, beaten
1   teaspoon vanilla or rum flavoring
2   cups Rice Krispies
2   cups chopped pecans
1   cup flaked coconut

Combine first 5 ingredients in a large saucepan and cook over low heat for 10 minutes, stirring constantly. Remove from heat, add cereal and pecans mixing well. Shape into balls and roll in coconut or shape into 2 logs and roll in coconut. Cool and slice thin.

DATE NUT ROLL

2   cups vanilla wafer crumbs
2   cups finely chopped pecans
1   8 ounce package chopped dates
¾   cup Eagle Brand condensed milk
1   tablespoon water

Combine all ingredients in a large mixing bowl, mix well. Divide mixture in half: shape each into an 8 x 1 inch roll. Wrap rolls in wax paper, chill overnight. To serve, slice as desired.

DATE ROLL

3   cups sugar
1   cup evaporated milk
3   tablespoons butter
3   tablespoons light corn syrup
1   cup chopped dates
1   cup chopped walnuts
1   teaspoon vanilla

Combine sugar, milk, butter, and corn syrup in medium saucepan. Over medium heat, bring to a boil, stirring, add dates. Boil to soft ball stage, 238 degrees on candy thermometer. Add walnuts and vanilla. Beat until thick, turn out on board and shape in two rolls, about 1 ¾ inches in diameter. Wrap in waxed paper. Place in refrigerator. Slice ⅓ inch thick to serve.

EASY OATMEAL COOKIES

2½ cups sifted all purpose flour
1   teaspoon baking soda
1   teaspoon salt
1½ teaspoons cinnamon
½   teaspoon nutmeg
¾   cup Crisco
½   cup granulated sugar
1   cup light brown sugar
2   eggs
¼   cup milk
2½ cups uncooked Quaker oats

Cream Crisco, sugars, eggs, and milk together well. Sift first five
ingredients together. Add to egg mixture and mix until smooth.
Stir in oats. Drop by teaspoons onto greased cookie sheet. Bake
at 375 degrees for 10 - 12 minutes. VARIATION: Use 1 cup
oats and one 12 ounce package of chocolate chips. 1 cup nuts
may also be added if desired.

FANTASY FUDGE

3   cups sugar
¾   cup butter
⅔   cup carnation evaporated milk
1   12 ounce package chocolate morsels
1   7 ounce jar marshmallow crème
1   cup chopped nuts
1   teaspoon vanilla

Combine sugar, butter and milk in a heavy 2 ½ quart sauce-pan. Bring to a boil, stirring constantly. Continue boiling on medium heat until it reaches a soft ball stage, 236 degrees. Stir constantly. Remove from heat, stir in chocolate pieces until melted. Add marshmallow crème, nuts and vanilla. Beat on medium until well blended. Pour into a buttered 13 x 9 inch pan. Cool and cut into squares. This can be cooked in microwave to prevent scorching, stir about every 2 minutes while cooking.

FRUIT CAKE SQUARES

6   tablespoons butter, melted
1½ cups Graham cracker crumbs
1   cup flaked coconut
1   cup chopped dates
⅓   cup flour to dredge fruit
1½ cups diced candied cherries
½   cup golden raisins
1½ cups chopped nuts
1   14 ounce can condensed milk

Pour melted butter into a 15 x 10 x 1 inch jelly roll pan. Sprinkle Graham cracker crumbs in pan and press to form crust. Layer ingredients by sprinkling coconut. Toss raisins, dates and fruit with flour and layer over coconut. Sprinkle nuts over top and press lightly to level mixture. Pour condensed milk evenly over top. Bake 20 - 30 minutes at 350 degrees. Cool and cut into squares.

GINGER SNAPS

¾   cup shortening
4   tablespoons molasses
2   cups self rising flour
1   teaspoon cinnamon
1   teaspoon cloves

1   cup sugar
1   egg
2   teaspoons baking soda
1   teaspoon ginger

Thoroughly cream shortening and sugar. Add molasses and well beaten egg. Add sifted dry ingredients and beat on medium until smooth. Roll into small balls and place 2 inches apart on greased cookie sheet. Bake at 300 degrees for 10 - 15 minutes.

GOFER BALLS

3 cups Graham cracker crumbs
½ pound melted butter
1 box 10 X powdered sugar
1½ cups flake coconut
1 cup chopped nuts
1 cup peanut butter
1 teaspoon vanilla
1 12 ounce package chocolate morsels
1 block paraffin wax

Mix butter and sugar well. Add other ingredients. Form into balls. Melt package of chocolate morsels and paraffin together in top of double boiler. Using a toothpick, dip balls into chocolate mixture and place on waxed paper.

GREAT COOKIES

1 box yellow butter cake mix
1 egg, beaten
1 stick butter
¾ cup chopped nuts

Mix together, roll and chill. Slice ¼ inch thick. Bake on greased cookie sheet for 8 - 10 minutes at 300 degrees.

HELLO DOLLY COOKIES

1   6 ounce package chocolate chips
1   cup graham cracker crumbs
1   cup coconut
½   cup butter
1   cup chopped nuts
1   can condensed milk

> Melt butter in a 9 x 13 inch baking pan. Sprinkle crumbs over melted butter: pour milk over crumbs. Top with remaining ingredients. Bake at 350 degrees for 25 minutes. Cool and cut into squares. VARIATION: peanut butter chips or butter-scotch chips.

JELLY COOKIES

3   sticks butter
3   egg yolks
2   teaspoons vanilla
1   cup sugar
5   cups plain flour

> Cream butter, add egg yolks, add remaining ingredients. Roll in small quarter size balls. Place on greased cookie sheet. Make a small indention in center of cookie, fill with jelly. Bake at 350 degrees for 10 - 12 minutes until lightly browned.

JIFFY DOUGHNUTS

1   can refrigerated oven ready biscuits
cinnamon
sugar
powdered sugar

> Cut a hole in center of biscuits with a thimble. Fry in preheated oil until golden brown, turning. Drain. Roll at once in granulated sugar and cinnamon combined or powdered sugar. Serve hot. BISMARKS: Fry refrigerated biscuits as above whole, do not cut out center. Cool slightly and cut a slit in the side of each biscuit. Slip a small teaspoon of jelly into the center and close tightly with finger. Roll in powdered sugar. Serve warm.

LEMON COCONUT BARS

1½ cups unsifted flour
½   cup powdered sugar
¾   cup butter or margarine
4   eggs, slightly beaten
1½ cups granulated sugar
1   teaspoon baking powder
½   cup real lemon juice
¾   cup flaked coconut

> In medium bowl, combine flour and powdered sugar. Cut in butter until crumbly. Press onto bottom of a lightly greased 9 x 13 inch pan. Bake at 350 for 15 minutes. In large bowl, mix eggs, granulated sugar, baking powder and lemon juice. Pour over crust, top with coconut. Bake 20 minutes or until golden. Cool. Cut into bars. Store in refrigerator.

LEMON MOUSSE

1   14 ounce can evaporated milk
1   cup sugar
juice from 3 lemons
1   grated rind of lemon
2   cups vanilla wafer crumbs, divided

       Place milk in a bowl in freezer until milk starts to freeze. Ice crystals will form around edges. Remove and whip until stiff: gradually add sugar and continue whipping. Add lemon juice and rind. Line bottom of an 8 inch square pan with 1 ¾ cups of vanilla wafer crumbs. Pour milk mixture over crumbs: sprinkle with remaining ¼ cup crumbs. Freeze. Cut in square and serve. Garnish with lemon slices.

LEMON SQUARES

1   cup all purpose flour
¼   cup sifted powdered sugar
½   cup butter
2   tablespoons all purpose flour
½   teaspoon baking powder

2   eggs, beaten
1   cup sugar
1   lemon rind, grated
3   tablespoons lemon juice

       Combine 1 cup flour and ¼ cup powdered sugar, add butter, mixing well. Spoon into a 9 inch square baking pan. Press into pan evenly. Bake at 350 for 18 - 20 minutes or until lightly browned. Combine 2 tablespoons flour and baking powder. Set a side. Combine eggs, sugar, lemon rind and lemon juice, beat well. Stir dry ingredients into egg mixture and pour over baked crust. Bake at 350 degrees for 25 minutes or until lightly browned and set. Sprinkle lightly with powdered sugar. Let cool and cut into 1 ½ inch squares. Yields: 3 dozen.

LIGHT-AS-AIR DIVINITY

2¼ cups sugar

½ cup light corn syrup

½ cup water

¼ teaspoon salt

2 egg whites

1 teaspoon vanilla

¾ cup chopped candied fruit

½ cup chopped nuts

STEP 1: In heavy 2 quart saucepan, stir together sugar, corn syrup, water, and salt. Clip candy thermometer to side of pan. Cook and stir over medium heat until sugar dissolves. Avoid splashing sugar on side of pan. STEP 2: Cook without stirring to 260 degrees or hard-ball stage. Remove from heat. Immediately, in large bowl, beat egg white at high speed with mixer to stiff peaks - tips stand straight. STEP 3: Remove the thermometer: gradually pour hot syrup in a thin stream over egg whites, beating at high speed. Add syrup slowly to ensure proper blending. STEP 4: Add vanilla and a few drops of food coloring, if desired: beat at high speed for 4 - 5 minutes until candy holds it shape when beaters are lifted, mixture falls in a ribbon, but mounds on itself. STEP 5: If candy is beaten enough, mixture will stay mounded in a soft shape when a spoonful is dropped onto waxed paper. If mixture flattens out, beat ½ to 1 minute more. The mixture is over beaten if it is stiff to spoon and surface is rough. If mixture is too stiff, beat in hot water, a few drops at a time, until candy is soft consistency. STEP 6: When candy holds its shape, stir in fruit and nuts, if desired: quickly drop candy by teaspoons onto waxed paper, or shape mixture into two 13 inch rolls with buttered fingers: roll in finely chopped nuts, coconut or crushed peppermint candy. Slice crosswise. Store tightly covered. NOTE: never double the recipe when

making divinity the mixture will not cook properly, and will be too much for the mixer to handle. When cooking, make sure the thermometer bulb is completely covered in the boiling liquid, and doesn't touch the bottom of the pan. Read the thermometer at eye level. Humidity affects the cooking of candy, so plan to make divinity on a relatively dry day. If you have to make candy on a rainy day or humid day, cook the candy 2 degrees higher than called for in the recipe.

LUNCH BOX BROWNIES

1½ cups butter

3 cups sugar

6 eggs

3 teaspoons vanilla

2½ cups all purpose flour

¾ cup cocoa

1 teaspoon salt

1½ cups chopped nuts

Cream butter and sugar in large bowl. Add eggs one at a time beating on medium speed after each. Add vanilla and mix well. Combine flour, cocoa and salt and add to creamed mixture. Stir in chopped nuts. Spoon into a greased and floured 13 x 9 x 2 inch pan. Bake at 350 degrees for 40 - 45 minutes or until done. Let stand 1 hour before cutting into bars.

MACAROONS

3	egg whites	1	cup sugar
1	cup coconut	3	cups cornflakes
1	cup nuts		

Beat egg whites until peaks form, add sugar slowly and beat until stiff. Fold in coconut, cornflakes and nuts. Drop by teaspoonfuls on greased cookie sheet and bake at 325 degrees for 20 minutes without opening the oven door. Cool before removing from pan.

MARSHMALLOW CRESCENT PUFFS

¼	cup sugar	1	teaspoon cinnamon
2	8 ounce cans Pillsbury	16	large marshmallows
	Crescent Dinner Rolls	¼	cup butter, melted

Combine sugar and cinnamon. Separate 2 cans crescent rolls into 16 triangles. Dip a marshmallow in melted butter: then in sugar - cinnamon mixture. Place marshmallow on wide end of triangle. Fold corners over marshmallow and roll toward point completely covering marshmallow. Squeeze edges of dough to seal. Dip point side in butter and place buttered side down in greased muffin tin. Place pan on cookie sheet while baking. Bake at 375 degrees for 10 - 15 minutes until golden brown. Immediately remove from pan and drizzle with icing.

ICING

| ½ | cup powdered sugar | 2-3 teaspoons milk |
| ½ | teaspoon vanilla | |

Mix together and blend until smooth.

MILLIONAIRES

1   14 ounce package caramels
1½ tablespoons milk
2   cups coarsely chopped pecans
1   12 ounce package chocolate morsels
1   block paraffin

Combine caramels and milk in top of double boiler: heat until caramels melt, stirring occasionally. Beat with wooden spoon until creamy, stir in pecans. Drop by teaspoonfuls onto buttered waxed paper. Cool. Combine chocolate and paraffin in top of double boiler: stir until melted. Dip each millionaire into chocolate mixture using a toothpick. Place on waxed paper to cool. NOTE: Caramels may be melted in microwave. Stir every 30 seconds until smooth.

MOCK PRALINES

½   cup sugar
2   sticks butter
1   cup chopped pecans
original Graham crackers

Line cookie sheet with foil, then line sheet with Graham crackers, broken apart. Put filling mixture in saucepan and bring to a boil. Boil exactly 80 seconds. Pour over cookies and bake 15 - 18 minutes at 350 degrees. Let cool and break apart.

NUTTY MARSHMALLOW LOG

2   cups chopped pecans
1¼ cups 4 X powdered sugar, divided
1   16 ounce package marshmallows
3-4 tablespoons peanut butter

Combine pecans and 1 cup 4 X powdered sugar, sprinkle evenly over a large sheet of wax paper. Melt marshmallows in top of double boiler or microwave. Stir in peanut butter. Pour mixture over powdered sugar pecan mixture. Mix with hands until pecans and sugar are blended into mixture and mixture resembles soft dough. Shape into 2 rolls, 1 inch in diameter. Let stand about 45 minutes. Roll in remaining powdered sugar, let stand 30 more minutes. Cut into slices. Store in covered container, separating layers with wax paper. Yields: 100 slices.

OATMEAL COOKIES

6   cups uncooked oatmeal
3   cups light brown sugar
3   cups butter, room temperature
3   cups plain flour, unsifted
1   tablespoon baking soda

Mix together well. Roll in very small balls. Butter bottom of a glass. Dip buttered glass in sugar and use it to flatten cookies. Bake on ungreased cookie sheet 10 - 12 minutes at 350 degrees.

OATMEAL KRISPIES

2	cups oatmeal
2	cups Rice Krispies
1	cup nuts
1	cup coconut
1	cup Crisco
2	eggs
1	cup brown sugar
1	cup white sugar
2	cups plain flour
1	teaspoon baking soda
½	teaspoon salt

Cream sugar and Crisco. Add eggs and beat well. Add sifted flour, salt and baking soda. Fold in other ingredients. Drop by teaspoonfuls on greased cookie sheets and bake at 350 degrees for 10 - 12 minutes.

OLD FASHION TEA CAKES

1	stick butter, melted
3	eggs, beaten
1½	cups sugar
1	teaspoon vanilla

Mix together until well blended. Sift self rising flour just like you were going to make biscuits. Make a well in center of flour. Using the above mixture make up just like you do biscuits. When dough is a soft ball, roll into 1 inch balls and place on greased cookie sheet 1 ½ inches apart. Flatten with fingers. Bake at 400 degrees until lightly browned, about 10 minutes.

ORANGE BALLS

2½ cups vanilla wafer crumbs
1   stick butter, melted
¼   cup undiluted frozen orange juice
1   cup 10 X powdered sugar

Mix all ingredients. Roll in small balls. Roll in more 10 X powdered sugar. Store in air tight container. Store in refrigerator. Yields: about 60.

PEANUT BUTTER BALLS

1   cup white Karo syrup
1   cup sugar
1½ cups peanut butter
6   cups cornflakes
1   cup finely chopped nuts

Bring sugar and syrup to a boil, remove from heat immediately. Add peanut butter, stirring to a smooth paste. Pour over cornflakes and nuts. Mix together, drop by teaspoon onto wax paper.

PEANUT BUTTER CANDY

1   24 ounce package white almond bark
1   cup creamy peanut butter
2   cups cocktail peanuts
3   cups miniature marshmallows
3   cups Rice Krispies

Melt bark and peanut butter over low heat. Can melt in microwave. Stir in remaining ingredients coating well. Drop by tablespoons onto wax paper. Cool and serve.

PEANUT BUTTER COOKIES

1   cup white sugar
1   cup light brown sugar
1   cup Crisco
1   cup peanut butter
1   teaspoon vanilla
2   eggs, beaten
2   teaspoons baking soda
3   cups cake flour
dash salt

Cream sugar and Crisco. Add peanut butter, vanilla and eggs. Mix until creamy. Roll into dime sized balls. Place on greased cookie sheet. Press down with fork in a criss cross design. Bake for 10 - 15 minutes at 400 degrees.

PEANUT BUTTER CUPCAKES
(Children Love Them!)

½   cup peanut butter
⅓   cup Crisco
1½ cups brown sugar
1   teaspoon vanilla
2   eggs
2   cups sifted all purpose flour
2   teaspoons baking powder
½   teaspoon salt
1   cup milk

Cream Crisco and peanut butter together. Gradually add brown sugar beating until light. Add eggs one at a time, beating on medium until fluffy: add vanilla. Add dry ingredients, which have been sifted together, alternately with milk. Blend well. Fill paper bake cups, in muffin pans, half full. Bake at 375 degrees for 15 - 20 minutes. Cool, frost with peanut butter if desired. Yields: 2 dozen.

PEANUT BUTTER FUDGE

3   cups sugar
¾   cup butter
⅔   cup carnation evaporated milk
1   12 ounce package peanut butter morsels
1   7 ounce jar marshmallow crème
1   cup chopped nuts
1   teaspoon vanilla

Combine sugar, butter and milk in heavy 2 ½ quart saucepan: bring to a boil, stirring constantly. Continue boiling over medium heat until mixture reaches soft ball stage, 236 degrees. Stir constantly. Remove from heat, stir in peanut butter morsels until melted. Add marshmallow creme, nuts and vanilla: beat well until well blended. Pour into a buttered 13 x 9 inch pan. Cool and cut into squares. You may cook in microwave, stir about every 2 minutes while cooking.

PEANUT BUTTER STICKS

1   loaf day old bread
2   cups smooth peanut butter
⅔   cup peanut oil
½   cup honey

Using an electric knife, cut trimmings off bread and save. Cut bread in ½ inch strips. Place bread strips on cookie sheet and bake at 250 degrees for 45 minutes. Mix peanut butter, oil and honey together until smooth. Dip baked bread strips in peanut butter mixture, rub off excess. Roll in bread crumbs that have been made from bread trimmings. Place on paper towels to dry overnight. Store in air tight container.

PECAN BRITTLE

2	cups chopped nuts	1	cup sugar
½	cup light Karo syrup	1	tablespoon butter
1	teaspoon baking soda	1	teaspoon vanilla

Mix together nuts, sugar, and syrup. Microwave on high 8 minutes. Stir in 1 tablespoon butter and 1 teaspoon vanilla. Microwave on high 2 minutes, 30 seconds. Quickly stir in 1 teaspoon baking soda and pour and spread over buttered cookie sheet. Let cool and break into pieces.

PECAN DREAMS

1ST LAYER

½	cup butter	1	cup cake flour less 2
¼	cup 4 X powdered sugar		tablespoons for 2nd layer

Mix butter, sugar and cake flour until thoroughly blended. Put in 11 x 15 inch pan.

2ND LAYER

2	eggs	1½	cups light brown sugar
2	tablespoons cake flour	½	teaspoon baking powder
1	cup broken pecans		

Beat eggs lightly. Add brown sugar, flour and baking powder sifted together. Mix until smooth. Add nuts. Spread on top of first layer. Bake at 375 degrees 30 - 40 minutes. Cut in squares.

PECAN KISSES

1   egg white
1   cup dark brown sugar
1   cup chopped pecans

Beat egg white until stiff: add sugar one tablespoon at a time until well mixed. Stir in pecans. Drop from teaspoon onto greased cookie sheet. Bake at 250 degrees for 30 minutes. Store in tight container after cooking.

PECAN PIE BARS

1   package yellow cake mix, reserve ⅔ cups
⅓   cup butter or margarine
1   egg

Mix together reserving ⅔ cups dry cake mixture for filling

FILLING
½   cup packed light brown sugar
1½ cups dark brown syrup
1   teaspoon vanilla
3   eggs
1   cup chopped pecans

Grease a 9 x 13 inch baking pan. Combine remaining dry cake mix, butter and 1 egg until blended. Press into bottom of pan. Bake at 350 for 15 - 20 minutes. In large bowl, combine reserved ⅔ cups dry cake mix, brown sugar, corn syrup, vanilla and 3 eggs. Pour over warm base. Sprinkle with nuts. Bake 30 - 35 minutes or until set. Cut into bars when cool.

PECAN CRISPIES

½   cup butter
6   tablespoons brown sugar
6   tablespoons granulated sugar
1   egg
½   teaspoon vanilla
1½ cups sifted all purpose flour
1   teaspoon baking powder
¼   teaspoon baking soda
¼   teaspoon salt
1   cup chopped pecans

Cream butter and sugar until light. Beat in egg and vanilla. Sift together dry ingredients, blend on medium into creamed mixture. Stir in nuts. Drop from teaspoon on ungreased cookie sheet. Bake at 375 degrees about 10 minutes. Cool cookies slightly before removing from pan. Yields: 2 ½ dozen.

PETITE CHEESE CAKES

2   8 ounce packages cream cheese
2   eggs
1   tablespoon lemon juice
1   tablespoon vanilla extract
¾   cup sugar
1   box vanilla wafers
your favorite pie filling

Mix all ingredients and blend well. Grease petite muffin tins and place one vanilla wafer in bottom of each. If wafer is too large, trim edges so it will fit flat in bottom of tin. Spoon cream cheese mixture over vanilla wafer, filling tin ½ full. Bake at 375 degrees for 15 minutes. Top with your favorite pie filling.

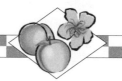

PINEAPPLE NUT COOKIES

½   cup Crisco
½   cup brown sugar
½   cup sugar
1   egg, beaten
2   teaspoons baking powder
½   teaspoon baking soda
½   cup crushed pineapple
1   cup chopped nuts
1   tablespoon lemon juice
2   cups cake flour
¼   teaspoon salt

Cream Crisco and sugar together, add egg and beat well. Sift dry ingredients together and add with well drained pineapple, nuts and lemon juice. Drop by teaspoonful onto a well greased cookie sheet. Bake at 375 degrees for 15 minutes. Yields: 48.

POPPY - COCK
(KARO CRAZY CRUNCH)

2   quarts popped corn
1⅓ cups pecans
⅔   cup almonds
1⅓ cups sugar
1   cup butter
1   teaspoon vanilla
½   cup white Karo syrup

> Mix popped corn and nuts and spread on cookie sheet. Combine sugar, butter, and syrup in a 1 ½ quart saucepan. Bring to a boil over medium heat stirring constantly. Continue boiling, stirring occasionally, 10-15 minutes or until mixture turns a light caramel color. Remove from heat, stir in vanilla. Pour over popped corn and nuts and mix to coat well. Spread out to dry. Break apart and store in air tight container.

POTATO CANDY

1   medium potato
peanut butter
powdered sugar

> Boil medium size potato in jacket. Peel and mash. Sprinkle with powdered sugar. This will make it liquid, but it thickens. Grease and flour wax paper. Roll out potato mixture and spread with layer of peanut butter. Roll up and slice.

QUICK AND EASY SUGAR COOKIES

½ cup butter
1 large egg
1 2.75 ounce package instant mashed potatoes

1 cup sugar
1 6 ounce package Bisquick
2 teaspoons vanilla

In large mixing bowl, cream butter and sugar until light and fluffy. Add egg and beat well. Stir in Bisquick mix and potato flakes. Add vanilla and blend thoroughly. Drop in 1 inch balls onto greased cookie sheet. Bake at 350 degrees for 10 - 12 minutes or until golden brown around edge.

RAW APPLE COOKIES

1¾ cups Crisco
½ teaspoon salt
½ teaspoon baking soda
½ teaspoon ground cloves
1 cup packed brown sugar
1 cup uncooked oats
1¾ cups red cooking apples unpeeled and chopped

1½ cups all purpose flour
½ teaspoon baking powder
½ teaspoon cinnamon
½ cup nuts
2 eggs
1 cup chopped dates

In mixing bowl, beat Crisco and sugar until creamy. Beat in eggs until well blended. Add dry ingredients, then oats, apples, nuts, and dates. Drop by teaspoonful on greased cookie sheet. Bake at 350 degrees 10 - 12 minutes or until lightly browned. Yields: 60.

SNOWBALLS

1	box vanilla wafers	½	cup butter
1	15 ounce can crushed	1	cup coconut
	pineapple, well drained	⅔	cup sugar
2	egg yolks	1	cup whipped cream
1	cup nuts		

Cream butter, sugar, egg yolks, pineapple and nuts. Put between two vanilla wafers. Freeze. Roll in whipped cream, then coconut. Freeze.

SOUR CREAM OVEN DOUGHNUTS QUICK AND EASY

2	cups Bisquick mix	¼	cup sugar
1	teaspoon ground nutmeg	¼	teaspoon ground cinnamon
½	cup sour cream	½	cup sugar
1	egg	3	tablespoons butter, melted
1	teaspoon ground cinnamon		

Mix biscuit mix, ¼ cup sugar, nutmeg, ¼ teaspoon cinnamon, sour cream, and egg until soft dough forms. Gently smooth dough into ball on floured board. Knead 10 times. Roll dough ½ inch thick. Cut with floured 2 ½ inch doughnut cutter. Lift doughnuts carefully with spatula and place about 2 inches apart on ungreased cookie sheet. Bake at 425 degrees for 8-10 minutes until browned. Mix ½ cup sugar and 1 teaspoon cinnamon. Immediately roll doughnuts in cinnamon and sugar mixture.

STRAWBERRY FLUFF

1   yellow cake mix
1   16 ounce Cool Whip
1   8 ounce sour cream
1   cup powdered sugar
1   cup milk
1   16 ounce package strawberry glaze
1   16 ounce package strawberries

Bake cake according to directions. Let cool and cut into small squares. Mix Cool Whip, powdered sugar, sour cream and milk. Pour over cake squares and let sit for 8 hours in refrigerator. Remove. Top with strawberry glaze, then add strawberries.

SWEDISH HEIRLOOM COOKIES

1   cup butter
1   cup powdered sugar, not sifted
½   teaspoon salt
1¼   cups pecans
1   tablespoon vanilla
2   cup sifted flour

Cream butter and sugar. Add other ingredients. Shape into balls and bake on ungreased cookie sheet for 15 - 18 minutes at 350 degrees. Yields: 4 ½ dozen.

SWEET POTATO MUFFINS

½ cup butter
2 eggs
1½ cups all purpose flour
2 teaspoons baking powder
¼ teaspoon nutmeg
½ cup chopped pecans

1¼ cups sugar
1¼ cups mashed
    sweet potatoes
¼ teaspoon salt
1 cup milk
½ cup raisins, optional

Preheat oven to 400. Cream butter and sugar. Add eggs. Blend in sweet potatoes. Mix in dry ingredients alternating with milk. Fold in nuts and raisins. Fill greased muffin tins ½ full. Bake for 25 minutes.

TEA TIME TASSIES

1 3 ounce package
   cream cheese
1 cup sifted all purpose flour

½ cup butter

Let cream cheese and butter soften at room temperature, blend. Stir in flour. Chill at least 1 hour. Shape into balls and press into bottom and onto sides of 1 ¾ inch muffin tins.

PECAN FILLING

1 egg
1 tablespoon soft butter
⅔ cup chopped pecans

¾ cup brown sugar
1 teaspoon vanilla
dash salt

Beat together on medium speed egg, sugar, butter, salt, and vanilla until smooth: stir in pecans. Put 1 teaspoon filling in each pastry cup. Bake at 325 degrees 20 - 25 minutes until filling is set. Remove from muffin tins and place on paper towel to cool.

TOFFEE CRUNCH BARK

1   cup light brown sugar
2   sticks butter
saltine crackers
1   10 ounce package peanut butter chips
1   cup chopped nuts

Place single layer of crackers on a 16 x 10 ½ x ½ inch pan. In microwaveable bowl, melt butter, add sugar, microwave for 2 ½ minutes on high. Pour over saltines. Bake at 350 degrees for 7 minutes. Remove and sprinkle 10 ounce package peanut butter chips and 1 cup chopped nuts. Spread over saltines. Place in refrigerator to cool. Break apart. Serve.

TOFFEE CRUNCH COOKIES

½   cup butter
1   box butter recipe yellow cake mix with pudding
1   cup pecans chopped
2   large eggs
1   tablespoon water
1   16 ounce bag brickle chips

Beat butter at medium speed with mixer until creamy. Add cake mix, eggs and water beating until blended. Stir in brickle chips and pecans. Drop cookie dough by tablespoons onto ungreased cookie sheets. Bake at 350 degrees for 8 - 10 minutes or until edges are browned. Top will look moist. Transfer to wire racks to cool. Yields: 4 dozen.

WHEATIES COOKIES

2 cups Crisco
1½ cups light brown sugar
1½ cups white sugar
2 cups plain flour
4 eggs
1¼ teaspoons salt
2 teaspoons vanilla
1 teaspoon baking powder
2½ teaspoons baking soda
2 cups coconut
5½ cups quick oats
5 cups Wheaties cereal, crunched

Mix sugars, Crisco, eggs and vanilla. Add dry ingredients. Drop by spoonfuls onto greased cookie sheet. Bake at 350 degrees 12 - 15 minutes. Yields: 5 ½ dozen. Freezes well.

THIS
and
THAT

Index

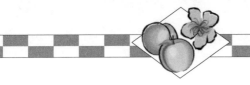

BAR B QUE SAUCE

18.5   ounce bottle Original Kraft
Barbeque Sauce
3.5   ounces lemon juice
hot sauce
red pepper
black pepper

> Pour bottle of Kraft sauce into sauce pan. Add lemon juice.
> Simmer over low heat. Add to personal taste, hot sauce, red
> pepper, black pepper.

BASIC WHITE SAUCE

2   tablespoons butter
2   tablespoons flour
½   teaspoon salt
1   cup milk

> Melt butter over low heat: remove from heat, add flour and salt.
> Stir until smooth. Return to heat and slowly add milk. Cook,
> stirring constantly until thick and creamy.
> VARIATIONS: cheese, add ¾ cup grated cheese to sauce, stir
> until melted. Creamy dill sauce variation, to white sauce, add
> ¼ cup sour cream and 1 teaspoon dried dill weed. Serve with
> vegetables or fish.

BUTTER CREAM ICING

½ cup Crisco Shortening

½ cup butter

1 teaspoon vanilla

4 cups sifted powdered sugar

Cream butter and Crisco with mixer. Add vanilla and sugar slowly. Mix until smooth and spread on cool cake. This is a great icing for any flavor cake.

CRISCO ICING

1 1 pound box 4 X powdered sugar

1 cup Crisco

1 teaspoon salt

½ teaspoon almond extract

4 tablespoons water

½ teaspoon vanilla extract

Mix together until creamy and smooth. Spread on cake.

CUCUMBER RELISH

1   gallon finely chopped cucumbers
1   quart finely chopped onions
1   cup finely chopped red bell peppers
1   cup finely chopped green bell peppers
1   cup finely chopped carrots
3   tablespoons pickling salt
3   cups vinegar
3   cups sugar
2   teaspoons ground turmeric
1   teaspoon whole cloves
2   tablespoons mustard seed
3   2 inch cinnamon sticks

Combine cucumbers, onions, peppers, carrots, and salt in large mixing bowl, mix well and refrigerate 8 hours or overnight. Drain. Tie spices in a bag. Combine spice bag, vinegar and sugar in a large saucepan. Bring to a boil. Add vegetables and boil gently, stirring often, for 15 - 20 minutes or until desired consistency. Put into hot sterilized jars and screw metal bands on tightly. Process in boiling water bath 15 minutes. Yields: about 6 pints.

DILL PICKLE

1   cup curing salt
2   quarts water
1   quart vinegar
½   box Sauers pickling spice
fresh garlic cloves
dill weed

Place cucumbers sliced or whole in sterilized jars. Put 1 clove garlic and few pieces of dill weed to each jar. Mix together the above ingredients in a heavy saucepan. Boil 2 minutes and pour over cucumbers. Seal jars.

GARLIC BLUE CHEESE BUTTER

4   fresh garlic cloves
½   teaspoon onion powder
½   teaspoon Montreal steak seasoning
½   cup butter, divided
4   ounces crumbled blue cheese ¾ cup
½   teaspoon dried thyme

Crush garlic, using garlic press, into microwave safe bowl. Add onion powder, steak seasoning, and 2 tablespoons of the butter. Microwave on high for 30 seconds or until butter melts. Stir and microwave 1-2 minutes, stirring once, or until hot and fragrant.

Let stand to cool completely, about 5 minutes. Cut remaining 6 tablespoons butter into small pieces: add to garlic mixture with blue cheese and thyme. Chill until ready to serve over savory steaks or fresh baked bakery bread. Yields: 8 servings.

GIBLET GRAVY

½   cup flour
⅓   cup juice from cooked turkey
2½ cups chicken broth pieces
2   hard boiled eggs, sliced into pieces
liver and gizzard chopped into small pieces

>   Mix together, simmer until thickened. Serve over cornbread dressing.

GRANOLA

8-10 cups one minute quick cook Quaker Oats
½   cup honey
3   cups soft dark brown sugar
3   sticks butter
1   cup coconut flakes
1   cup raisins

>   Melt butter in a large pan. Add sugar and honey. Stir in oats and coconut. Add enough oats to soak up all the sugar mixture, don't have the mixture too wet. Spread mixture onto two baking sheets. Bake at 375 degrees till brown and drying 20-30 minutes. Turn oat mixture 3 times during cooking time using a fork to brake into lumps.

ITALIAN PICKLED PEPPERS

3   large bell peppers: green, red, and yellow
1   3 ounce can anchovy fillets
6   sprigs parsley
3   cloves garlic
6   cups vinegar
1½ cups water
1½ cups sugar
1   tablespoons salt

> Wash peppers, remove core and seeds. Cut into eighths. Pack in hot, clean jars. Into each jar put 1 anchovy fillet, one sprig parsley, and ½ clove garlic. Combine remaining ingredients and pour into jars to within ½ inch of the top. Seal jars. Process in hot water bath for 30 minutes. Yields: 6 pints. Note: a couple of slices of jalapeno peppers to each jar gives it "character."

LEMON SAUCE

1   cup sugar
2   tablespoons cornstarch
2   cups water
¼   cup butter
2   tablespoons lemon juice with rind

> Mix sugar and cornstarch over heat. Gradually add water. Boil 1 minute. Stir in lemon juice and butter. Yields: 2 cups. Great served over gingerbread or pound cake.

PICKLED OKRA

4-4½ pounds small okra
7   cloves garlic
7   hot peppers
7   teaspoons dill seed
1   quart vinegar
1   cup water
½   cup pickling salt

Wash okra well, drain and set aside. Place 1 clove garlic and 1 hot pepper into 7 half pint jars. Pack jars firmly with okra leaving ½ inch head space. Add 1 teaspoon dill seed to each jar. Combine vinegar, water and salt in large pan, bring to a boil and pour over okra. Seal jars and process 10 minutes in boiling water bath. Let stand 5 weeks before opening.

TOMATO SAUCE

20 large tomatoes
6   medium onions, chopped fine
3   hot peppers, chopped fine
3½ cups vinegar
3   tablespoons salt
4   cups sugar

Mix all ingredients and cook until thick. Put in sterilized jars and seal.

WATERMELON RIND PICKLE

Prepare rind by removing all red fruit and green peel. Make sure rind is firm, or pickles will look puffy. Cut in desired pieces. Soak overnight in lime water solution using 1 tablespoon lime to a gallon of water. Be sure rind is covered in lime water. In the morning, remove rind from water and rinse well. Cook in clear water until tender — about 1 hour. Drain. In large pan mix sugar and vinegar. 2 cups sugar to 1 cup vinegar. Place drained rind in this. Be sure rind is covered with vinegar and sugar solution. Cook until rind looks glassy — 1 hour. Add 1 teaspoon oil of cloves and cook 30 minutes longer. Pack in sterilized jars. Add 1 piece of stick cinnamon to each jar. Be sure rind is covered with solution. Note: Oil of cloves is strong. Use 1 teaspoon to one large rind.

MY FAVORITE HOUSEHOLD HINTS

1. To remove clorox or onion odor from hands — run a stainless steel table knife blade over hands while holding under running cold water.

2. For quick relief for a burn, grab the toothpaste tube and rub a thin layer of toothpaste over the burn.

3. To remove ink marks from garments, spray hair spray on the mark before laundering.

4. A little cooking oil or butter put in water for spaghetti, noodles or rice will prevent it from sticking together.

5. When baking pies, put a strip of aluminum foil around top of the crust to keep from getting the crust too brown. Remove foil for last 10 minutes of baking.

6. You can remove chewing gum from a child's hair by rubbing with a dab of peanut butter.

7. A little salt sprinkled in the frying pan will keep fat from spattering.

8. If you don't use a whole jar of pimentos, put the remaining part in a small jar and cover with vinegar and refrigerate. They will last a long time.

9. To prevent discoloration when you boil cauliflower, put a squirt of lemon or a teaspoon of vinegar in the water.

10. Baking soda or cornmeal will remove grease spots from carpeting. Pour a generous amount over the spots and brush lightly. Leave overnight and vacuum off the next day.

11. Another remedy to remove ink marks from garments, soak in milk before laundering.

12. To remove sticky price stickers — rub with peanut butter.

13. To remove grape juice stains — rub with men's shaving cream.

14. Treat bee stings with meat tenderizer. Another remedy for bee stings, spray with WD40.

15. Peanut butter will get scratches from CD's. Wipe off with a coffee filter.

16. Wine stains, pour on Morton salt and watch it absorb into the salt.

17. To remove crayon marks from the wall, rub with toothpaste.

18. Gatorade is good for migraines. Power Ade won't work.

19. Dirty Grout — Listerine

20 Grass Stains — Karo Syrup

INDEX

Index

To order additional copies, make checks payable to:
Father & Son Publishing, Inc. and mail to:
4909 North Monroe Street ♦ Tallahassee, Florida 32303

Please send me _____ copies of *Southern Favorite Receipts Volume 2* @ $19.95 plus $3.00 each for postage and handling. Florida residents add 7% sales tax. Enclosed is my check or money order for $_____

Name _____

Address_____ Phone _____

City_____ State _____ Zip _____

MasterCard/Visa Card # _____CV Code _____

Exp. date _____ Signature _____

- -

To order additional copies, make checks payable to:
Father & Son Publishing, Inc. and mail to:
4909 North Monroe Street ♦ Tallahassee, Florida 32303

Please send me _____ copies of *Southern Favorite Receipts Volume 2* @ $19.95 plus $3.00 each for postage and handling. Florida residents add 7% sales tax. Enclosed is my check or money order for $_____

Name _____

Address_____ Phone _____

City_____ State _____ Zip _____

MasterCard/Visa Card # _____CV Code _____

Exp. date _____ Signature _____

- -

To order additional copies, make checks payable to:
Father & Son Publishing, Inc. and mail to:
4909 North Monroe Street ♦ Tallahassee, Florida 32303

Please send me _____ copies of *Southern Favorite Receipts Volume 2* @ $19.95 plus $3.00 each for postage and handling. Florida residents add 7% sales tax. Enclosed is my check or money order for $_____

Name _____

Address_____ Phone _____

City_____ State _____ Zip _____

MasterCard/Visa Card # _____CV Code _____

Exp. date _____ Signature _____

- -